THE HEALTHY
Donkey

THE HEALTHY
Donkey

Sarah Fisher & Trudy Affleck

THE CROWOOD PRESS

First published in 2016 by
The Crowood Press Ltd
Ramsbury, Marlborough
Wiltshire SN8 2HR

www.crowood.com

British Library Cataloguing-in-Publication Data
A catalogue record for this book is available from the British Library.

ISBN 978 1 78500 171 0

Photographs by Bob Atkins and Sarah Fisher

Dedicated to all donkeys, and to those who love and care for them

Typeset by Jean Cussons Typesetting, Diss, Norfolk

Printed and bound in India by Replika Press Pvt Ltd

Contents

Introduction

Greet every day with enthusiasm
Be loyal to those you love
Share good things with close friends
Be kind
Take a moment to weigh up your options if something bothers you and know when it is time to fight,
flight or stand your ground
Be gentle
Spread humour and joy whether at work or at play
Be strong yet sensitive in equal measure
Have patience with those around you
Be wise
Be true
Be Donkey

We both have many years of experience interacting and living with donkeys and make no apologies for being totally captivated by these intelligent, entertaining, affectionate and peaceful animals. We are not just lovers of our own donkeys; we are passionate ambassadors for each and every one. We wanted to write this book to give you some new ideas and perhaps deeper insights into the wonderful world of donkey guardianship, and to share seventy-five techniques and tips that have enabled us to help donkeys lead happy and fulfilling lives.

In our opinion, there are few greater things in life than the companionship of donkeys and we know we are not alone in this belief. Whether you are only just discovering the delights of sharing your life with these incredible beings, are in the process of offering a home to some of the unwanted donkeys currently in need, or are already experienced in many aspects of donkey management and care, we hope you will enjoy exploring rewarding ways of looking after, and connecting with, your glorious donkey friends.

PART 1

1 Living with Donkeys

A BRIEF HISTORY OF THE DONKEY

The donkey has played a vital role in the history of man, yet there has been minimal research into the domestication of the donkey over the years. A study exploring the origins of the modern donkey (Kimura *et al.*, *Ancient DNA from Nubian and Somali wild ass provides insights into donkey ancestry and domestication*), however, has concluded that the Nubian ass and a second, potentially extinct, subspecies are the ancestors of the modern donkey. The Somalian ass has been ruled out as a contributor to the domesticated donkey's gene pool.

Analysis of genetic data from modern donkeys reveals the Somali wild ass has considerable mitochondrial divergence from the Nubian wild ass and domestic donkeys; it is no longer considered to be an ancestor.

Despite relatively limited available genetic data, evidence from archaeological sites suggests that domestication of the wild donkey, well adapted to arid environments, began approximately five thousand years ago in Africa, enabling early societies to become more mobile, increase trade and spread further afield. The discovery and analysis of ten donkey skeletons buried in Egypt about 3,000 BC (Rossel *et al.*) confirmed that donkeys were used as beasts of burden in Egyptian society, with the skeletons showing wear and tear consistent with carrying heavy loads.

In an article entitled 'Evaluating the Roles of Directed Breeding and Gene Flow in Animal Domestication', Fiona B. Marshall et al. examine the domestication and management process of the donkey and highlight the important role that donkeys continue to play as working animals in the lives of African pastoralists today. The article illustrates how the donkey's long gestation rate, resilience, ability to range widely in search of a mate and use as a means of transport over significant distances all contributed to limited directed breeding; historically herders relied in part on wild and feral donkeys for herd growth, as opposed to actively managing reproduction.

It is thought that the domestic donkey was brought to the United Kingdom by the Romans. Over the centuries the European donkey has been used in agriculture, as a means of transport, for the production of mules and by the military, but as technology advanced, so the working donkey became largely redundant. Changes in agricultural practice have had a devastating impact on many donkey breeds; of the 162 official breeds of donkey worldwide,

The small stature, intelligence and friendly character of the Miniature Mediterranean donkey make them ideal family companions, provided they are given appropriate outlets for their natural drives and desires.

only five are not endangered, and six are sadly already extinct (Rischkowsky & Pilling, 2007).

European donkeys were probably introduced to the Americas by Christopher Columbus in the fifteenth century and by Spanish conquistadors in the sixteenth century. They were used as working animals and for breeding mules, and the trend continued through subsequent centuries with large numbers of donkeys being imported during the gold rush in the nineteenth century. They lost their value as working animals following the introduction of the railways and the end of the mining era.

In Europe small breeds like the Miniature Mediterranean donkey, found in Sardinia and Sicily, were used to turn grinding stones and transport water. Larger breeds, such as the distinctive French Poitou and the now rare Spanish Andalusian donkey, were used for the production of large working mules. Although the Miniature Mediterranean is in decline in its native countries, this delightful breed can be found in the USA, Canada, the UK and other European countries thanks to Roger Green, who imported a small herd into the USA in the 1920s. Roger Green is quoted as saying 'Miniature donkeys possess the affectionate nature of a Newfoundland, the resignation of a cow, the durability of a mule, the courage of a tiger and an intellectual capability only slightly inferior to man's.'

There are an estimated 40–50 million donkeys in the world today, the majority of them working animals essential to the success of many communities worldwide, providing low-cost power and transport. The robust, endearing donkey has stamina, is relatively easy to manage, utilizes feed more efficiently than a horse of comparable size, is patient, and tolerates thirst better (and rehydrates more quickly) than horses or oxen. With the majority of specific breeds in sharp decline, it is the mixed breed, standard donkey that is now most commonly kept both as a working animal and as a pet.

DONKEY GUARDIANSHIP

Donkeys come into people's lives for a variety of reasons, and once they become a part of your family you will quickly realize what amazing creatures they are. Donkey guardianship can be addictive and time spent in their rewarding company is never wasted. A happy contented donkey makes a calm, kind, patient, loving companion and one that will most certainly make you smile.

Donkeys are highly adaptable and can turn their hoof to a wide variety of skills, including being ridden and driven, as willing teachers in therapeutic equine programmes, protecting livestock, trekking, pulling a toboggan through the snow, carrying shopping or feedbags using pack saddles, or simply enjoying being fussed and groomed to help ease the trials of the human day. Donkeys may be strong and resilient but they are also highly intelligent, sensitive animals that enjoy companionship. They are entertaining and expressive, and if a donkey appears to be miserable or depressed, it is more likely to indicate poor management or ill-health rather than his general temperament. Donkeys tend to stop and process information and may shut down when overwhelmed, and it is this response that gives donkeys the unfair reputation of being stubborn.

A well socialized donkey is a joy to own and will often seek out human company. Donkeys have a natural curiosity and really enjoy being a part of the social scene. A happy donkey will often leave the pleasures of the pasture to interact with humans and, provided they enjoy contact on their body, will willingly line up to be groomed and fussed without the need to be caught and held or tied. They love to learn and, regardless of whether you decide to train your donkey to be ridden, driven or to compete in-hand, the relationship between you will be enhanced if you invest time in teaching him some solid life skills and give

A happy, contented donkey will seek out human company. Having the opportunity to hang out with these incredible animals is one of life's greatest gifts.

him the necessary mental stimulation using techniques based on mutual cooperation, kindness and trust.

Their intelligent, independent and gregarious nature means that donkeys are easily bored; if left to their own devices, or simply turned out in a barren field day after day, they may well find their own entertainment. Providing a safe, enriched environment for your donkey, and ensuring that his needs are met, will minimize the chances of him developing behavioural problems linked to frustration.

Rough and tumble games can be an important part of a donkey's life. Donkey geldings in particular will often engage in boisterous interactions with each other. Large rope dog toys, wellington boots, small branches pulled from the hedgerows or anything that

can be picked up and incorporated into a game of tug of war will be used. Horse balls and rubber feed bowls can also provide donkeys with great stimulation but may not survive the rigours of donkey play. A new pristine feed bowl can be shredded in minutes and even a heavy water container filled to the brim and wedged securely into a tyre will be effortlessly flung around the stable with great gusto if your donkeys like to play. Make sure that any toys you offer to your donkeys are safe. Remove any buckles from Wellington boots and avoid items that might have sharp edges or loops that could get caught on the teeth and around the hooves and legs.

A significant amount of time can be spent watching two donkey geldings engrossed in a game. Some games can get quite rough and

Rough, physical games are a natural behaviour, particularly when the donkeys are young. Provided the companions graze calmly together and share the same housing quite happily at all other times, a robust playfight is no cause for concern.

may even appear to be getting out of hand; many a new donkey owner worries that their donkeys are fighting in earnest, and bite marks on the neck, legs and flanks as a result of rough games are not uncommon. However, where several donkeys are kept together it is important to ensure that bullying is not taking place.

Like all animals, donkeys have individual personalities and different capabilities, and they process training at different speeds. Some are naturally more outgoing, while others may be a little more introverted. All donkeys, however, thrive in a teaching environment employing methods tailored to their individual characters that enable them to use their brains. They can learn new skills at a very fast rate when reward-based techniques such as clicker training are used. Clicker training is not a necessary part

of donkey education but it can add variety to the way you interact with your donkey and can certainly be a useful resource in your teaching tool kit in addition to the tips we have shared in this book. It can help a donkey develop pleasant and rewarding associations with something that may have caused anxiety in the past.

Using food rewards as part of a teaching exercise is not the same as giving regular tidbits from the hand. Over-treating donkeys can encourage them to become pushy and to bite; this is unfair to the donkey and unpleasant for the human and can cause a break-down in the bond between donkeys and their carers if the donkey is reprimanded for this easily avoidable behaviour. This is of particular importance where children are concerned. A happy donkey is usually gentle with children and can become a much valued friend to every member of the family but it is important that all interactions with children are monitored and, above all, safe.

It is natural for children to want to participate in feeding animals but it is better to encourage them to hide carrot peelings around the field before the donkeys are turned out, or to mix them in with the feeding straw in the stable before the donkeys are brought in, rather than offering treats by hand.

TO BREED OR NOT TO BREED

There are few things in life more heart-warming than the sight of a donkey foal and the temptation to breed from a beloved donkey can be immense, but the harsh reality is that there are countless unwanted donkeys suffering appalling neglect and even death as a direct result of over-breeding.

While some well-bred donkeys may still command a reasonable price, and the rarer breeds would certainly benefit from well managed breeding programmes, there are many unwanted mixed breed donkey foals, jennies and jacks across the western world that are surplus to requirements. Seeing adverts for donkeys and foals on offer for a few pounds or free 'to a good home' is heart-breaking, and we live in an age where life is cheap. Do not be fooled into purchasing a pair of breeding donkeys in the hope that there can be some financial remuneration. The costs involved in caring properly even for little donkeys are significant (more so if you do not own your

It can be tempting to over-handle donkey foals. Quiet interactions from an early age help the donkey develop good life skills, but too much fussing and petting can create problem behaviours as the youngster starts to mature.

Breeding from your donkey is a big responsibility. Unless you have taken on an unwanted jenny that is already in foal, diligent research beforehand and the support of an experienced breeder will minimize the risks of problems arising during birth and throughout the donkey's life.

own land) and the day-to-day expenses, if the donkeys are to be well looked after, cannot be recouped through the sale of one top-class foal.

Jacks should ideally be cared for by people with some experience. They require careful management and handling to prevent them from causing problems created by testosterone, breeding when too young or covering a jenny that is not mature enough to withstand the rigours of carrying a foal full term. Donkeys are

talented escape artists and think nothing of climbing over or under fencing if the motive to do so is high. We recommend that any male donkey not destined to be used in a breeding programme is gelded. Though some jacks may be small in stature, they are still stallions and a high skill level is required to ensure safety for all concerned as even the most quiet- tempered, gentle jack can change dramatically if an in-season jenny is close by. A gelded donkey will have more freedom, will be less frustrated and will generally be easier to handle and train – and thus able to live a more fulfilling life – than an entire jack in the wrong environment.

Good genes and careful planning cannot safeguard the future for any animal. Circumstances change, and with the majority of rescue organizations overwhelmed with ever-increasing numbers of donkeys in need coming into care, there are simply not enough homes or resources to support all the unfortunate donkeys that fall upon hard times. In short, the western world does not need any more poorly bred donkeys, so please think long and hard before embarking down this road.

Donkeys have a relatively long lifespan and, even if you are confident that you can keep the foals you intend to breed, please bear in mind your donkeys might outlive you. While the average life of a donkey in the UK is around twenty-seven to thirty years, a healthy donkey could potentially live for over forty years. If you do decide that you want to pursue the delights of donkey breeding, consider setting aside some money in a no-risk savings plan to support your donkeys if your own situation changes. If you cannot afford to put aside some money to protect your donkeys' future, it might be best not to bring any more lives into the world. If you can set aside some money, make sure that you have discussed your plans with every family member. It may be your children, friends or relatives who will inherit the donkeys that you choose to breed, or step in to care for

them if you become unwell. As guardian of any animals, it is wise to make provision for them in your will.

If you do choose to explore the option of breeding from your donkey, get advice from experienced, registered breeders. Any animal used for breeding, whether it be a jenny or a jack, should be of top quality, with a good temperament, good health and excellent conformation. It can be hard to be objective when you have an emotional attachment to an animal and, unless you are experienced, you may not recognize what constitutes good conformation, so get your donkey assessed by someone in the know. If you are advised not to breed from your donkey, then don't!

If you have thoroughly considered all the salient points with regard to breeding and decide to go ahead, do your research first. Read as much as you can on the subject of breeding and select a well-bred registered jack with good blood lines. A reputable breeder will not let their stud donkeys cover a poor quality jenny, so be wary of anyone who offers a jack for stud services without asking questions prior to covering. Avoid breeding from a jenny before she reaches physical maturity, which is around five to six years of age, and spend time working with her to ensure that she is comfortable being handled, stabled and led in a variety of situations. While donkeys can, and do, breed from a younger age, the impact of carrying a foal to full term can have a detrimental effect on a young jenny's health and development.

2 Husbandry

Every experienced donkey guardian appreciates that donkeys are not small horses with long ears. True, there are some similarities between donkeys and native ponies, but there are also many differences between these two members of the equine family. This can take horse owners by surprise when they first interact with donkeys, particularly if their equestrian experience is limited to a handful of different breed types.

Donkeys can, and do, live quite happily in the company of horses but their dietary and management requirements are not the same as those of the majority of their equine cousins, and this fact should not be overlooked. Regardless of whether the donkey is a Miniature Mediterranean or a Mammoth, they all require understanding, adequate shelter whether it be a stable or covered dwelling, a place to roll, companionship ideally

If resources are limited, donkeys will lead a solitary life in the wild but the domestic donkey generally prefers the company of at least one friend.

with a fellow donkey, human interaction and an appropriate diet.

Donkeys also differ from horses in terms of physiology and anatomy, and in their responses to some equine medications. They generally have a higher resting respiratory rate and rarely show the more obvious signs of pain. If veterinary treatment is necessary, it is important that the attending vet understands the differences between these two wonderful members of the equine family.

COMPANIONSHIP

Donkeys are gregarious animals and need the company of at least one friend. In general, your donkey will prefer to have another donkey of the same sex as a companion. Paired donkeys will happily share a feed bowl, and will usually graze side by side or in close proximity to each another. Males and females can live together but some geldings that are turned out with female donkeys of breeding age may become rather thuggish when the jenny comes into season. Jennies may also mount each other at this time.

Donkeys forge firm bonds with their companions and some can become distressed and depressed if parted and may even panic, even if they are only separated by a stable door. This can be a challenge if one donkey requires veterinary attention or cannot engage in rumbustious activities as a result of injury or disease.

The exercises in this book can help to increase self-confidence so that donkeys paired together become less dependent on each other for emotional security. We are not suggesting for one minute that confident donkeys can then be housed alone as companionship is vital, but should the need arise one donkey can be given individual time without inciting panic in their friend.

BODY SCORE

Body scoring provides a way of assessing the physical condition of a donkey. A donkey with a body score of one would be considered to be in poor condition and a donkey with a body score of five would be considered obese. The ideal condition score is three.

A donkey with a condition score of three will have a light covering of muscle and fat on the neck, and the ribs will be just covered by a layer of fat/muscle so that the ribs can be felt with light pressure. He will have good muscle cover on the hindquarters and the hip bones will be rounded in appearance and, as with the ribs, can be felt with light pressure.

Establishing a balance between restricting grazing and providing sufficient exercise and mental stimulation for their donkey to maintain a good body score is an on-going challenge for most donkey guardians.

DIET

Donkeys originated in dry desert countries such as Africa and Asia and have evolved to survive in that type of environment. This can cause problems for donkeys living in a wetter climate with constant access to lush grasslands; this is a common issue in the UK. With diligence and careful planning, however, donkeys can lead long and healthy lives in a variety of climates.

Their origin means that donkeys' nutritional requirements are considerably less than those of a pony of comparable size. In their native desert environment donkeys eat a mix of dried vegetation from small bushes and other scrub, and are constantly on the move in search of food. Prolonged turn-out in pastures with limited exercise and constant access to rich grass can be detrimental to their health.

Donkeys can become obese very quickly and may develop fatty crests along the neck and fat

This delightful and very happy donkey, now in the care of RSPCA Lockwood, has a fallen crest. Donkeys can develop fatty pockets in the neck due to metabolic problems or as a result of being overfed.

pads on the body and hindquarters, which can be hard to shift. The fatty pads may also calcify (harden) despite appropriate weight loss that may be achieved through suitably controlled feeding and care.

If the donkey's diet is deficient in any way, he may be desperate to consume far more food than his body actually needs. The provision of a good equine mineral block in the stable or the field shelter will give him access to the nutrients he requires without the need for additional supplements in feed. Personally we prefer plain mineral blocks, not tubs that contain molasses.

If your donkey is lacking essential minerals in his diet, you may notice that he tries to eat the block instead of licking it from time to time. If he continues to do this over a period of time, please consult your veterinary surgeon who can run some blood tests to ensure that your donkey does not have any underlying health concerns.

Mineral blocks developed for equines (not cattle) can be left in a bowl on the floor of a stable or the shelter but if your donkeys throw their water around and generally make a mess, you can install a low-level holder to keep the

mineral block clean. Check the holder regularly for signs of chewing.

Donkeys are trickle feeders and will spend a great proportion of their day eating. Restricting access to grass is important, particularly during the spring and summer months, but they must have a high fibre food source readily available.

Extreme weight gain or excessive weight loss can cause serious medical problems that can prove fatal. If your donkey is overweight, look at ways you can change your management and feeding routine to achieve and maintain a healthy body score. Implement any necessary dietary changes gradually over a period of a few weeks and, if your donkey is rather portly, look at ways you can lower the calorie intake in an appropriate way rather than imposing a strict starvation regime which could be detrimental to your donkey's health and well-being.

In the UK donkeys do well on a diet of barley straw, supplemented with grass hay if necessary, and with restricted access to fresh, lush grass. They require little in the way of supplement to this basic diet. A feed balancer can be added to ensure that the diet is not lacking in essential nutrients, but unless the donkey is old, unwell, in foal or lactating, additional feed is seldom required. Some grass hay may be necessary during the winter months but ad lib barley straw should ideally make up a substantial part of their diet.

If you cannot find a supplier of good quality barley straw, oat or wheat straw can be fed to provide the high fibre diet that donkeys require. Oat straw has a higher calorific value than barley straw and wheat straw is more fibrous, so you will need to take your donkey's individual needs into account. Older donkeys with poor teeth will probably do better on oat straw with additional grass hay if required, while wheat straw will probably be best suited to younger donkeys that have good dental health.

If good quality straw is in short supply or if your donkey is underweight or has trouble eating due to dental issues or ill-health, try feeding a mix of un-molassed chaff with high fibre cubes. If you do need to provide extra feed, source products suitable for laminitic equines or produced specifically for donkeys. Soak the feed to reduce the risk of choking if your donkey bolts his food or struggles to chew appropriately.

As natural browsers, donkeys enjoy having access to suitable, non-toxic, cuttings from hedgerows or logs from trees such as hawthorn, ash or beech and will spend several hours stripping the bark from the stems. Grass cuttings must not be fed, however, as they can cause colic. Vegetables are a much healthier treat option than sugary snacks, and donkeys enjoy pieces of carrots, apples, banana and root vegetables such as swede or turnips, particularly

As browsers, donkeys love to strip bark from logs and trees. The provision of non-toxic logs helps to wear the incisors appropriately, while offering natural enrichment.

Donkeys love to problem-solve. Offering safe toys and containers in which food can be hidden will give your donkeys fun and rewarding mental stimulation and satisfaction.

through the winter months when fresh grass is not available. Make sure that any vegetables or fruits you feed your donkeys are fresh, and do not overfeed them.

If your donkeys are stabled, feeding straw from mangers is safer than using a haynet. Donkeys love to problem solve; enrichment that extends feeding time and satisfies a donkey's inquisitive nature can be provided by placing several footballs on top of the straw in the manger so that the donkey has to push the balls around in order to get to the straw to feed. Make sure he is confident enough to push the balls around. Hiding carrot peelings in the straw will also give the donkey something to do while stabled.

Always ensure that anything you feed your donkey is high quality. Mouldy or dusty hay, straw or feed will have a detrimental impact on your donkey's health.

WATER

Donkeys may not consume much water in comparison to horses but they do need access to fresh water at all times. Avoid using brightly coloured water buckets that attract bugs, and remember that donkeys do not like stale water – they will avoid drinking water that has stood in the stable overnight. Even if your donkeys do not drink much water, it is advisable to refresh the water supply on a daily basis in both the paddock and the stable and ensure that water troughs are kept clean.

Some donkeys do not like drinking excessively cold water. Monitor the amount of water drunk through the winter months and if you notice that your donkey's water consumption has decreased during chilly weather, offer a bucket of slightly warm water to see if that is more acceptable.

If you take your donkey out and about to shows or other events, remember to take a container of water from your own yard. Many animals prefer to drink water from home when they travel.

HOUSING

The donkey's coat is not waterproof and their hooves are porous. Some donkeys do not mind being out in the rain, but constant exposure to wet conditions can compromise their immune system and give rise to respiratory problems, skin diseases such as rain scald, and fungal conditions such as thrush that are detrimental to hoof health.

Providing a place to shelter from the weather and flies is an important part of donkey care.

Appropriate shelter for your donkeys is an important part of their management and care. As well as providing a place to dry out, access to a shelter will offer shade and the opportunity to escape from flies during the warmer summer months. If your donkeys are affected by midge bites, you may need to adapt their turn-out routine during spring, summer and early autumn as midges are most active at dawn and dusk.

Regardless of the type of shelter provided, good drainage and good ventilation are important. The shelter needs to be large enough to accommodate the number of animals that will be using it, with ample space for each donkey to lie down should they so choose, and should be enclosed on at least three sides, facing away from the prevailing winds.

Some donkeys may not be accustomed to being stabled and will prefer a shelter that allows free access to outside space, while others enjoy coming into a stable to rest at night or during the day. It is important to restrict access to grazing if your donkeys live in an area where the pasture is rich, but with good planning it can be relatively easy to provide your donkeys with access to shelter combined with an opportunity to play and browse outside.

If your donkeys are going to be stabled at times, the doors need to be of a height that enables each donkey to see over his door so that he can watch what is going on, but be mindful that a donkey that has been moved into a new environment may jump over a low stable door if he feels unsafe or lonely.

BEDDING

As well as being a main source of food, barley straw makes excellent bedding for donkeys. Some donkeys tend to eat their bedding regardless of what it is, and barley straw is the safest bedding for them to ingest. If you cannot locate barley straw for bedding, you may need to experiment before finding an alternative that your donkeys will not eat. Ensure that any straw you use is of good quality and discard any bales that are dusty or mouldy.

Rubber matting can be a useful base on which to put a thick layer of barley straw and provides additional insulation from cold concrete floors in the winter months. There are many different grades of rubber matting on the market and it is well worth investing in heavy, robust matting if your donkeys like to play. Light cushioned matting can be shredded quite quickly and even though a committed donkey can move even heavy duty matting with relative ease, it is more likely to remain intact should it be utilized as a tuggy toy and dragged around.

TURN-OUT AND FENCING

Donkeys are highly adaptable and can live in a variety of environments. Feral donkeys, presumed to be the descendants of abandoned working animals, can be found in several countries, including Cyprus, the USA, Mexico, parts of the Caribbean, Italy and Australia.

Wild and feral donkeys range for miles, which naturally wears down their hooves and soles, and provides mental stimulation as well as plenty of exercise. A lack of opportunities to engage in natural activities and limited exercise can cause behaviour problems in domesticated donkeys through boredom and frustration. Poorly managed and inappropriate pasture can also have a detrimental effect on their well-being. It is the responsibility of the guardian of any animal to provide an appropriate, safe,

Wild donkeys roam through historic Cripple Creek, Colorado. They are probably direct descendents of working donkeys that were liberated when the miners left the area.

enriched environment to ensure that natural behaviours, drives and desires can be fulfilled.

As a general guide, two domestic donkeys can be kept for every acre of available pasture but this will depend on several factors, including the size of the donkeys (to a degree), their age and personalities, the layout and quality of the pasture (both rich and poor), daily management and lifestyle of the donkeys, and the availability of other facilities such as a covered yard, and so on.

If grazing has to be restricted through the spring and summer and during wet winter months, the provision of a large covered area or access to a safe yard with hard standing and shelter will give your donkeys the opportunity to stretch their legs, roll and engage in games. Remember that donkeys are naturally inquisitive and may play with anything that is left lying around.

Rolling in dust provides donkeys with insulation against heat and cold in their native desert environment and a domestic donkey will relish the opportunity to enjoy a good roll in the dirt.

Wooden structures may be viewed as a delicacy by some donkeys, particularly youngsters, and post and rail fencing, timber stables, gates and posts may be chewed. If you share your life with an enthusiastic wood gnawer, try to ensure that it is not a response to factors such as an inappropriate diet, boredom or dental problems. Bear in mind that wood chewing is normal donkey behaviour, however, and try to provide him with some logs from non-toxic trees instead to give him a less costly alternative. If you are unsure which trees and shrubs are safe for browsing donkeys, be diligent with your research and take expert advice from reliable donkey specialists; never follow well intentioned but potentially fatal tips from novice owners.

Anti-chew products may be off-putting for some donkeys but they do not always deter a keen wood chewer. Post and rail fencing is expensive to install and can quickly be destroyed by a gnawer. Once you have ruled out all possible contributory causes and supplied other sources of wood, if your donkey persists with chewing the fencing you may have to resort to installing a line of electric fencing inside the perimeter of the field to protect the boundaries and keep your donkey safe. Please note, however, that electric tape or rope should be used with caution where foals are concerned.

As donkeys are both browsers and grazers, hedging may not be suitable as the only boundary to a field, especially if the hedgerow is sparse or not yet fully established.

If you are planning on breeding from your donkey, ensure that the perimeter of the field is suitable. Foals can easily crawl or roll under fencing designed for larger equines, and additional rails placed low to the ground will help to keep your little donkeys safe and secure.

Horse netting can help to keep roaming dogs out of paddocks if footpaths cross the land on which your donkeys are kept, but small donkey hooves can easily become entangled in the netting. If your paddock is netted, or if you need to keep dogs out of your pasture, you can create a safer environment by nailing additional planks of wood or half-round rails to the posts.

Strip grazing is one way of limiting grass intake, as is bringing the donkeys into a stable or yard for part of each day, but an alternative method is Jamie Jackson's Paddock Paradise system. This provides a track around the outside of the field, which helps to maximize the distance the donkeys walk while turned out, simultaneously minimizing their access to new grass. Depending on the size of the field, the area in the centre can be cut for hay, grazed by other animals such as sheep or perhaps a jenny with a foal, or used to give limited timed access to grass should any of the donkeys need additional feeding.

This system can be further enriched with the provision of a rolling area, appropriate logs for gnawing, and feeding stations filled with barley straw sited around the track. If you do install a track system, remember to provide some shelter and ensure the track is wide enough in places for the donkeys to engage in physical games.

Using the track system, it is quite possible to keep four medium-sized donkeys on just over an acre of field, with access to the track from April to the end of November and access to the middle of the field and the track from December through to March.

Whether donkeys are kept in a paddock with strip grazing or on a track system, regular picking-up of dung is an important part of parasite control, along with regular worm counts and an appropriate worming regime.

GENERAL HEALTH

A donkey's natural stoicism can make it difficult for owners to know when something is amiss, although an experienced guardian may detect some small change in the donkey's behaviour that sets alarm bells ringing. Low-grade colic,

back or neck pain and lameness (including laminitis) can be easily overlooked.

Regardless of the underlying medical problem that might be causing the distress, the most common signs that a donkey is unwell include: standing quietly at the back of the stable or in the field, low ears, lethargy, lack of vocalization, a dull or 'hard' eye, reluctance to play, disinterest in companions and/or surroundings, reluctance to eat, concern about being touched, aggressive behaviour, and changes in eating or drinking habits. Other more specific indicators of ill-health can be a change in droppings and urine, pale gums, a runny nose, rasping breath, and so on.

Hyperlipemia, also known as hyperlipidemia, is a severe metabolic disease that can affect donkeys following dramatically reduced food intake. It is caused by abnormally high levels of fat in the blood and can be fatal.

If your donkey displays any change in his normal behaviour, is off his food or exhibits any signs of distress, immediate veterinary attention is required.

GROOMING AND CARE

As well as being an important part of health care, grooming plays a role in building, and deepening, the relationship between you and your donkey. It enables you to check for body sensitivity and to develop trust. If your donkey has areas on his body that trigger a reaction when brushed, something is amiss. It may be that he is sore, is carrying tension, has matts in his coat that cause discomfort when the hair is pulled, is nervous or simply lacks good body awareness.

Slicker brushes designed for use on dogs are excellent tools to use on donkeys that are starting to shed their winter coat. Rolling is an important part of a donkey's life, and dust, debris from bedding, grass seeds, mud and so on can become trapped in the coat. The

Soft rubber groomers help to remove debris in the coat and increase circulation through the skin. They contour to the hand and to the donkey's body and can be an effective tool for helping donkeys overcome any grooming concerns.

slicker brush can help to remove dead hair and dislodge any matter, and the majority of donkeys really enjoy being groomed with this type of brush, provided the teeth of the brush are not pressed into his skin.

Soft rubber groomers are an excellent addition to any grooming kit as they shape to the contours of the donkey's body as well as to your hand, and can be used all year round. They are particularly useful when brushing areas where there is less protective muscle under the skin, such as around the donkey's face. This type of groomer is usually far more acceptable to a sensitive donkey than the more traditional dandy or body brush, as it is softer and cannot be gripped too tightly, thus automatically reducing the amount of pressure you might inadvertently apply when brushing.

If you cannot groom a donkey in your care or if he has no-go areas, use the Tellington TTouch® body-work exercises listed in the third section of this book to release tension and build confidence and trust. TTouch has helped countless animals worldwide to overcome grooming concerns. If you have taken on a

donkey whose coat is thickly matted, try using a warm, slightly damp (not wet) face cloth to increase the circulation to his skin and gradually loosen any dirt that may be adhering to his coat. This approach can be particularly helpful when working with donkeys with matted hair on their sensitive ears, provided the weather is not too cold.

If you use a hard-backed brush, be careful not to bang your donkey with the edge of the brush. Pay attention to the speed of your strokes and the pressure you are using, as well as his body language as you groom. If he fidgets, moves away, pins his ears or tightens his chin he is letting you know that he is unsure or uncomfortable, or that you are being too vigorous or perhaps simply rushing. Grooming should be something that he really enjoys, rather than an experience he merely tolerates or loathes.

If you are the guardian of a male donkey, sheath cleaning will also be an integral part of his health care; if you share your life with a jenny, cleaning her udder may be necessary from time to time as well.

Stallions and geldings produce normal secretions from sebaceous glands in the skin of the sheath and penis. When this combines with naturally sloughed skin cells, a waxy substance known as smegma is formed. It can be moist or dry and crusty, and the amount of build-up will vary from donkey to donkey. Accumulation of smegma can cause irritation and attract insects, and in extreme cases may even change the way the donkey walks as excessive, dry, crusty smegma can cause discomfort. When smegma accumulates around the urethral opening, a 'bean' can form which can affect the donkey's ability to urinate.

Jennies may also become itchy around their udders due to an accumulation of dust and dirt and irritation from insect bites. If you notice that your jenny is rolling or rubbing her tail excessively, check her udder for any debris or skin conditions that might be contributing to these behaviours.

Preparation is vital for either cleaning task as some donkeys dislike contact with the sheath and udder. If you cannot touch your donkey on his/her belly and inside the hind legs, it is less likely they will tolerate any gentle washing of these sensitive areas. Over-washing of the sheath is to be avoided and appropriate cleansing products designed specifically for this task should be used as soap can cause further irritation to delicate skin.

If you notice black, greasy marks on the inside of the hind legs it is highly probable that your donkey needs his sheath cleaning, but even if you do not notice any obvious signs you should still check for a build-up of smegma from time to time. You can use the TTouches listed in the body-work section to help your donkey remain relaxed and to accustom him to being handled around this area.

Donkeys are incredibly dextrous and rarely miss their mark if they kick out when feeling threatened, so enlist the services of a willing friend who can help you keep your donkey quiet and calm. Never punish your donkey

if he suggests, however strongly, that you need to stay well away from his private parts. If he becomes really agitated at the mere thought of you approaching him with soft sponges, warm water and a cleaning product, he may need to be sedated. Should he need to be sedated for any dental work, take the opportunity to check and clean his sheath at the same time.

FEET

A donkey's hooves are perfectly engineered to enable him to range for miles over rough, dry terrain and remain sound. The hooves are tougher, yet more flexible, smaller and more upright than those of the majority of other equines. Less obvious differences include a more concave, thicker sole, smaller bones, and a frog that extends further rearward.

If the hoof is balanced, the frog will be symmetrical in appearance and in contact with the ground. An uneven or misshapen frog can be indicative of an uneven foot. The frog, along with other structures in the foot, aids with

Foot abscesses are usually characterized by sudden-onset lameness. They are a common problem for donkeys that are exposed to consistently wet ground and those that are under par.

blood circulation in the hoof and lower limb when the donkey is on the move.

Abrasion from consistent movement over such terrain wears both the sole and the hoof wall, but on softer ground less wear occurs and this can cause a serious problem for donkeys that are left out in pasture without appropriate care.

Foot care is paramount to ensure that good hoof balance is maintained. If the foot is in good health, the hoof should be trimmed every six to ten weeks. If the foot is abnormal, more frequent attention may be required. The growth rate of the foot is affected by several factors, including

nutrition, conformation, injury, time of year (there is less growth in the winter), weather, environment, work and age.

An unbalanced foot will have a detrimental impact on the rest of the body and on physical health. Just as the angle and shape of the hoof will affect every other joint and influence muscle development, injury to any part of the body can change the appearance of the hoof due to changes in the way the donkey's weight is distributed through the limbs.

As well as regular visits from a farrier, daily management, including picking out the hooves, is an integral part of foot care. It is important that donkeys have access to hard standing

The angle of the left foreleg and hoof growth have altered following changes in this donkey's neck. X-rays showed a narrowing between two cervical vertebrae but it was the sudden difference in hoof growth that raised the alarm.

Many donkeys that come into welfare centres have been neglected in the past but with appropriate care and management dental issues such as these do not have to have a detrimental impact on their well-being.

during wet weather or if they are kept in damp climates so that their feet have a chance to dry out.

TEETH

Like his equine cousin the horse, a donkey's teeth need regular checking by either a vet or an equine dental technician as the adult teeth continue to erupt for many years. Donkeys are stoical and can continue to eat without apparent discomfort, even if their teeth are causing considerable pain.

Regular check-ups by a trained equine dental technician or vet every six to twelve months, depending on the age and health of the donkey and the condition of his teeth, are advisable to prevent the risk of dental issues causing distress and ill-health. The earlier a problem is detected, the easier it will be to address.

Adult donkeys can have up to five types of teeth – incisors, canines, pre-molars, molars and wolf teeth – although their actual dentition will vary depending on the individual animal. The incisors are the front teeth and are used to nip vegetation, strip bark and tear grass, as well as for biting as a means of expression, self-defence or in play. If access to grazing and browsing has been limited for any reason, the incisors may become excessively long, which will change the balance of the entire mouth.

Pre-molars and molars, also known as cheek teeth, are used to grind the food prior to swallowing. Canine teeth, sometimes referred to as tushes, are present predominantly in males, but can also be found in some females. They are located in the interdental space between the incisors and the pre-molars on both the upper and lower jaw, and are used during fights to hold and tear. They do not erupt continually as do the incisors, pre-molars and molars, but can become incredibly sharp. Long canine teeth can cause injury and can also get caught on objects

such as stable door bolts, and can sometimes crack, causing considerable discomfort. Some canine teeth never fully erupt and remain below the gums.

Wolf teeth are vestigial pre-molars and may be present in both male and female donkeys. They vary in shape, location and size but are most commonly found in front of the pre-molars on the upper jaw. Like the canines, wolf teeth may remain below the gum line in some instances.

Teeth that do not erupt are called 'blind' teeth, and the presence of blind wolf or canine teeth can cause considerable discomfort due to sensitivity in the gums. If you do not intend to bit your donkey as part of his education, it is not necessary to remove the wolf teeth but if you have plans to bridle your donkey for leading, riding or driving, seek the advice of your vet or equine dental

If your donkey has worn, missing or loose teeth he may need additional soaked feed as his ability to pick and chew grass, hay or barley straw effectively may be limited.

technician as wolf teeth can interfere with the bit and cause pain.

Dental imbalances can arise for a variety of reasons, including poor conformation, poor posture, injury, old age, poor management and so on. If there is uneven dental wear due to sharp edges, retained caps (baby teeth that did not shed), hooks, steps (where one pre-molar or molar is longer than the other teeth, usually as a result of a missing or broken corresponding top or bottom tooth), a wave (where two or more pre-molars or molars are higher than the other teeth) and so on, the natural, circular, grinding eating pattern of the donkey will be interrupted and cause further imbalance as the teeth will continue to erupt unevenly. Dental discomfort and diseases may also be caused by broken, missing or loose teeth, periodontal disease, diastema (a gap between teeth where food can become trapped), abscesses and so on.

As well as ensuring that your donkey receives regular attention from a dental specialist, spend time watching him eat. If he has good dental health you should notice that his mobile lower jaw (mandible) moves rhythmically both clockwise and anticlockwise to grind the food matter between the surfaces of the upper and lower cheek teeth.

Signs that your donkey may be in need of dental attention include up and down chewing as opposed to grinding, eating with a partially open mouth, dropping food, packing chewed food between the cheek teeth and cheek to prevent discomfort caused by sharp outside edges, smelly breath, slow or picky eating, reluctance to eat, a dull coat, weight loss, obesity, undigested food matter in the droppings, reluctance to be caught and behavioural changes when being led, ridden or driven and so on. It is important to remember, however, that many donkeys with severe dental problems continue to eat and may not display any obvious signs of distress when handled due to their stoical nature. Pay attention to his subtle 'language' as you approach your donkey with the headcollar or bridle and as you tack him up, and be mindful of his behaviour and the quality of movement when he is ridden or driven to ensure that any potential discomfort caused by the presence of dental issues is not overlooked.

3 Anatomy, Posture and Behaviour

Many of the exercises, tips and techniques included in this book are based on Tellington TTouch, also known as TTEAM, which stands for Tellington TTouch Equine Awareness Method. This unique approach to training and handling animals can have a profound and potent effect on the nervous system and improve physical and emotional well-being.

You do not need to have an in-depth knowledge of anatomy and physiology to be a good donkey guardian, but a condensed overview can help you understand why

Even if you are short of time, you can still utilize all your interactions with your donkey and teach him to slow, flex left and right, halt and walk on when coming in from or going out to the field.

incorporating TTouch into the day to day management, handling and education of your donkey can be so beneficial. Increased knowledge can also give you some insight into why he may be struggling in the world that humans have created for him. It can help you to understand the relevance of the inextricable link between posture and behaviour, and show you how you can improve your donkey's balance and well-being with the simple body-work and ground-work exercises described in this book.

When working with a donkey it is important to see things through his eyes. Always ask yourself what you think the donkey might be learning from the experience, whether you are bringing him in from the field, picking out his hooves, teaching him to lead, working through the steps to trailer loading, starting him under saddle or preparing him to be driven.

Think about how you can make every part of his education rewarding and fun, and help him to develop trust in you and in what you are asking him to do. In a nutshell, an animal feels either safe or unsafe, and there are many reasons why an animal may feel unsafe. A donkey that is confident in some situations may not necessarily be as confident in every other situation. Be aware that when we change one thing, we potentially change everything. Even the introduction of a new headcollar can elicit a temporary fear response regardless of the number of years a donkey has been happily wearing his old one.

Your donkey may have developed a fear of the known if he has been exposed to unpleasant experiences in his past, or have a fear of the unknown if his life experiences have been limited. Some donkeys may have been rushed through the early steps of learning and never fully processed what was being asked of them. Signs that they were struggling may have been overlooked. If you are taking on an older donkey, bear in mind he may behave completely differently once you get him home.

He may have been taken away from his friends, and be thoroughly confused by the change. He needs time to get used to the new sights, sounds and smells so be patient and allow him to settle and bond with his new companion(s), both two-legged and four.

Fearful animals often have quite specific postural traits and donkeys that consistently find it hard to adapt to new situations are often concerned about being touched around the ears, the face, the mouth, down the lower legs, and around the hindquarters and tail. They may also be braced in the neck and tense through the back. Releasing tight muscles, encouraging the donkey to lengthen and soften through the top line, relax through the tail, and enjoy contact on his extremities through gentle body-work and quiet ground-work can help a nervous donkey become more consistent and more considered in his responses. Even if he is naturally more sensitive, the TTouch exercises will help him to settle more quickly should something cause him concern.

It is not possible to control every aspect of the environment in which your donkey lives, but you can influence how he processes external stimuli and reacts to noise, movement around him, containment, being touched and so on by giving his nervous system new experiences, building confidence and by improving his balance and posture.

A donkey that is worried may shut down. If your donkey will not do something that you are asking him to do, it is more likely that he can't rather than won't and he needs time to process and evaluate the situation. It is this response that gives donkeys the reputation of being stubborn. While they may startle and run away before turning to face a perceived threat, or run backwards, they will often shut down and become immobile when unsure, overwhelmed, tired or anxious. Donkeys also have a tendency to stand and stare at whatever is causing them concern. When a donkey is worried or overwhelmed, he cannot learn.

Donkeys use their ears and eyes to gather information from their surroundings but they also use their nose. Allowing them to sniff novel objects, pathways, people and so on will enable them to build confidence and trust.

BASIC ANATOMY AND PHYSIOLOGY

Studying the function of the nervous system and gaining even a little knowledge of anatomy can be fascinating and illuminating. These are complex subjects that can be rather overwhelming, so here we have simplified some basic information on these topics that we think will be of interest; it certainly influences the way we understand and work with our donkeys.

The donkey's skeleton provides the framework of his body and is part of a skeletal system composed of ligaments, tendons, cartilages, bones and the membranes that cover the bones.

Formation and development of the bones is largely influenced by genetics, health and nutrition but can also be affected by exercise. Regular turn-out of young donkeys is crucial to ensure healthy skeletal development through appropriate, natural movement but a young donkey engaged in physical work too early may suffer long-term physical effects resulting from excessive strain placed on the maturing skeletal system.

Congenital problems or accidents do not have to limit a donkey's ability to lead a happy and fulfilling life. Although it may not be possible to influence what has happened in the past, you can change the impact it has on your donkey's future.

The lifespan of a working donkey is approximately twelve years. Jalala, a rescued working donkey with an injury to his left foreleg, has a brighter future thanks to the care of Dr Mujtaba and other members of the dedicated team at Nowzad in Afghanistan. (Photograph courtesy of Nowzad)

Bone is living, growing tissue that stores minerals and is constantly renewed through a process called remodelling. Red and white blood cells are produced in the bone marrow. As well as providing a framework for the attachment of muscles and other tissues, bones have important functions depending on their type and location; irregular bones of the spinal column protect the spinal cord, flat bones such as the skull and ribs protect vital internal organs, long bones such as those found in the limbs act as levers and aid locomotion, short bones such as the carpal bones allow for complex movement and help to absorb concussion, and sesamoid bones work in conjunction with the tendons to prevent the tendons coming into contact with bone.

The skeleton is divided into two main sections: the axial skeleton and the appendicular skeleton. The axial skeleton is composed of the bones of the head (including the bones of the ear and the hyoid apparatus), the vertebral column, the sternum and ribs, and the appendicular skeleton is composed of the fore- and hindquarters.

Donkeys do not possess a collar bone and the shoulder blades are held in place by muscles and tendons. The shoulder blades meet the thoracic vertebrae to form the withers. The hind limbs attach to the axial skeleton via the pelvis.

The donkey skeleton is similar to that of a pony, but there are some notable differences. Donkeys have one fewer lumbar vertebra and generally have a less pronounced wither than the majority of equines, the bones in the foot are smaller and variations in the number of sacral vertebrae have also been recorded.

The muscular system controls every movement of the donkey's body, both internally and externally. While the skin is the biggest piece of connective tissue, the muscles combined form the greatest tissue mass. There are three types of muscle: skeletal, smooth and cardiac. Smooth and cardiac muscles are involuntary, meaning that they function automatically. Smooth muscle is found in and around all the internal organs, such as the bladder and the digestive tract; cardiac muscle is thick, fatigue-resistant muscle found in the heart. Skeletal muscle is voluntary. It supports the skeleton, creates and controls movement, maintains joint stability and provides protection for the skeleton and internal organs.

Skeletal muscles have a 'belly' and attach to bones via tendons at each end. They are formed from thousands of muscle cells known as fibres, which are bound together by connective tissue.

There are different types of muscle fibres: slow twitch (type 1) and fast twitch (types 2a and 2b). Slow twitch muscles (type 1) contract slowly and are able to maintain this contraction for some time without fatigue. They are mostly used in low intensity exercise that requires stamina and endurance but low speed and low power. Fast twitch muscles (type 2b) are suited to short bursts of maximum speed and power, such as jumping and galloping. Type 2a fast twitch muscles fall between type 1 and type 2b.

All equines have a mix of muscle fibres but the ratio differs between species, between breeds and from equine to equine within each breed. Not surprisingly, donkeys have a lower percentage of fast-twitch muscles than horses (Valberg & Macleay, n.d., 2).

Tendons are tough bands of connective tissue and are designed to stretch only a little. They transmit force between the bones and the muscles. Ligaments are made of the same tissue as tendons. They connect the bones to each other and help to stabilize the joints. Soft tissue injuries occur when there has been excessive strain on the muscles, ligaments or tendons. They are more common in working donkeys, but can be caused by accidents or by poor posture and/or conformation.

Activation of skeletal muscle is controlled by the peripheral nervous system.

THE NERVOUS SYSTEM

The nervous system is a network of nerve cells and fibres that coordinates voluntary and involuntary actions, and transmits information to different parts of the body. It is processing internal and external information all the time, and therefore learning is also taking place all the time.

The nervous system is divided and subdivided into different parts. Every part of the nervous system is connected and nothing works in isolation.

Central nervous system (CNS)

The central nervous system controls and coordinates movement, action, decision-making and responses to the environment. It comprises the brain and spinal cord and is the centre of the body's communication system, processing and integrating information received from all parts of the body.

Peripheral nervous system (PNS)

The peripheral nervous system is made up of nerves leading to and from the central nervous system, and relays information to and from the CNS through this efficient and effective network. It controls movement, posture and reflexes, and processes sensory information.

The PNS is further divided into two major parts called the somatic nervous system (SoNS), associated with voluntary movement of the body, such as walking, turning the head and so on, and the autonomic nervous system (ANS), associated with involuntary movement, such as the beating of the heart, digestion, and so on.

The ANS is important to consider when working with any animal as it is subdivided into three further parts, but our main interest is in the two branches called the sympathetic nervous system (SNS) and the parasympathetic nervous system (PSNS).

Sympathetic nervous system (SNS) and parasympathetic nervous system (PSNS)

The sympathetic nervous system activates what is often simply referred to as the flight/fight reflex but an animal's natural responses to fear, increased arousal and stress can also include freeze, fidget/fool around, and 'faint'. These five main instinctive reactions to stimuli are often called the five Fs. They are preceded by more subtle nervous system responses that indicate the animal is becoming increasingly concerned, but the relevance of these more subtle signals may be inadvertently overlooked or ignored, or the animal's stress levels may rise so quickly that the smaller signs go unnoticed. Whatever the reason for these behaviours, it is important to remember that they are automatic responses to fear and not a conscious choice.

Always remember that an animal feels either safe or unsafe, and when we interact with them in any way it is our responsibility to ensure that they are never pushed to the point where their survival responses kick in. Many donkeys that show significant anxiety in one situation will

Yawning, licking and chewing, scratching and so on are nervous system responses and are signs that the parasympathetic nervous system is engaged. This can be triggered by a stressful or exciting situation or may be observed as the donkey starts to relax.

usually display smaller and perhaps less obvious concerns in other aspects of their life. If time is taken to address the small worries and increase the donkey's levels of confidence all round, the bigger worries will start to diminish and in many cases may disappear completely without any need to focus on the most visibly apparent cause for concern.

Sympathetic nerves originate in the spinal

There is always a good reason for 'bad' behaviour. Getting after a donkey that displays what we might consider to be antisocial responses will break down the bond.

cord. Donkeys that carry tension through the back, particularly the lumbar area, can be more reactive and instinctive in their responses than donkeys that are more relaxed through the body. Many animals that carry tension through the back respond in the same manner, regardless of where they evolved on the food chain.

It is really important to remember that a donkey that becomes concerned when handled, bucks when something touches him on the back, panics when asked to move through or into a narrow space, shuts down and stops when being led, moves around or kicks out when a leg is picked up by the farrier or when having his hooves picked out, becomes defensive in the stable, on the yard or in the paddock, and so on, is responding out of fear.

Punishing a donkey for this survival response will only increase that fear, create more stress and inhibit the education of the donkey. Remember: an animal that is afraid cannot learn.

It is far kinder, safer and more effective to use techniques that help to address and not suppress these instinctive responses by building confidence, releasing tension and influencing another part of the autonomic nervous system: the parasympathetic nervous system.

The parasympathetic nervous system is associated with rest and digestion, and restoring calm. It is activated in response to stressors that have triggered the sympathetic nervous system and enables the body to return to a state of balance.

Simple body-work exercises such as stroking the ears can help to lower the heart rate, slow respiration and improve digestion. Signs that the parasympathetic nervous system is at work include calm movements of the mouth such as slow licking and chewing, relaxation of the body, deep, rhythmical breathing, and slow blinking.

It is not just the digestion of food that occurs when the parasympathetic nervous system is engaged. Information can be processed too, and a donkey that is calm and happy in his day to day life and work will be easier to handle and teach as he will be willingly engaged in every interaction.

The nervous system needs time to process and absorb new information. Several short teaching sessions with plenty of breaks in between are therefore far more beneficial than one long session and it is often during the breaks that most learning occurs.

Think of the nervous system like a pervious rock beneath which sits the 'well of knowledge'. Imagine education is like drops of water. Drip feed new information and give it time to trickle through the pervious rock so that it can be collected in the reservoir below. Too much input in one go will flood the system and a high proportion of the information will be lost as it dissipates across the surface. Withholding good life experiences will leave the well of knowledge dry.

ENDOCRINE SYSTEM

The endocrine system controls hormone production and secretion, and can be likened to the PNS as both coordinate and control internal function. Hormones are naturally occurring chemicals that influence mood, behaviour, health, metabolism and development, and can be activated by both good and poor experiences, physical stress and physical well-being, and the way we interact with an animal.

It isn't necessary to have an in-depth knowledge of the endocrine system in order to work effectively with animals but awareness of the impact that external stimuli can have on the production and secretion of hormones can give us a better understanding of how we can help maintain a healthy lifestyle for our four-legged friends.

Donkeys are without doubt highly intelligent animals, but many of their responses to potentially alarming situations are instinctive and therefore automatic. The donkey is not choosing to be deliberately difficult if he struggles in new situations or is anxious about a visit from the farrier, for example. Fear is one of the primary causes of unwanted behaviours in all animals and can trigger the production of adrenalin – a hormone secreted by the adrenal gland. It increases the rate of blood circulation and respiration, prepares muscles for exertion and is produced in both high stress and exhilarating situations. Adrenalin can increase strength, block pain and heighten the senses, increasing hearing, sensitivity to contact, and influencing vision. It also has an impact on balance and spatial awareness.

High adrenalin is not always expressed in fast movement. A donkey that is shutting down or has gone into freeze may still have rapid respiration and rising adrenalin. Pain can trigger adrenalin, as can anxiety and fear. Regardless of the reason behind any increase in adrenalin, it is important to remember that adrenalin blocks an animal's ability to learn.

Gentle, non-threatening contact on the body can increase oxytocin. Oxytocin is also referred to as the trust or cuddle hormone and helps to override the flight/fight response and lower adrenalin. It is a myth that touching a fearful animal reinforces the fear. Mindful, gentle contact can override instinctive responses, and help an animal learn due to the effect that rewarding contact can have on the nervous and endocrine systems.

THE SENSES AND SENSORY INTEGRATION

Donkeys are visually aware and have excellent hearing. They can move their glorious ears to pinpoint the source of a sound and can detect the smallest change in their environment. They also have a keen sense of smell and will use their noses to explore new items, other animals and people.

Adrenalin heightens all the senses and a donkey that exhibits a change in behaviour is either unwell or has been alarmed by something that may not be obvious to us. If he is suddenly reluctant to be caught, starts rushing in-hand, when driven or under saddle, displays aggressive behaviour, or is hesitant to walk his usual route to or from his pasture perhaps, he is not being deliberately difficult or stubborn. Something has triggered concern.

New feed bowls and buckets may be viewed with suspicion if they smell strongly of plastic or rubber, or are a different shape or colour from those used previously. New gravel in a gateway, the introduction of a smart new headcollar or lead rope, a rustling jacket or headwear that changes the appearance of a trusted guardian are just some of the things that can cause consternation to a donkey, although it will generally be short-lived. As humans we tend to be less aware of subtle changes in our environment and may not fully appreciate the impact they can have on our donkey friends.

The senses work together, and sensory experiences include touch, movement, sight, sound, the pull of gravity, smell, taste and body awareness. The processing function of the sensory system that organizes and interprets this information is called sensory integration and it provides an important foundation for learning and behaviour. Animals with good sensory integration tend to be more confident and more sociable than animals with poor sensory integration.

Many donkeys that are sensitive to contact are also sensitive to sound. Sensory integration can be improved through gentle body-work, the use of additional techniques such as a body wrap (a simple stretchy bandage) that influences the tactile part of the sensory system,

The position of a donkey's ears will often correspond with the direction in which he is looking.

and in-hand leading exercises over different surfaces and ground-work equipment.

BALANCE AND PROPRIOCEPTION

We often hear the phrase 'it's in his head' when equines are difficult to manage but in our experience a high proportion of behavioural concerns in donkeys are linked to physical problems or areas of tension in the body. Physical, mental and emotional balance is linked.

Many donkeys that are concerned about being touched, are tense through the body and lack good body awareness find it hard to adapt to new situations and may appear to be slow learners. Inflexibility in the body can be linked to inflexibility in the mind and many animals

that are labelled as intolerant or difficult have restricted movement through their body. Rather than trying to train unwanted behaviours out of the donkey, it is far more rewarding and appropriate to address the reasons why the donkey may be struggling and to set him up for success by helping him move, and therefore learn, with ease. Even if donkeys do not exhibit any behavioural concerns, good physical health can minimize the risk of injuries, and ensure that the donkey is comfortable and content.

We pay great attention to quality of movement and teach our own and client donkeys to lead from both sides. A high proportion of quadrupeds load the left foreleg and are often stiffer through the diagonal right hind leg. Of course, some donkeys load the right foreleg and are stiffer on the left hind leg, and some load both the fore and hind limbs on

Maybelle is croup high following a growth spurt and carries tension through her back as a result. She struggles when being led across unlevel pasture.

Teaching Maybelle how to organize her body more effectively and keeping educational sessions short and easy to process will help support her through this developmental phase.

the same side, but the most common pattern tends to be left fore, right hind. Only leading a donkey from his left side can exacerbate this natural tendency. Indeed, many donkeys stand with their neck slightly flexed to the left even when they are at liberty. Bridles and headcollars that have buckles on the left side reinforce habitual handling from the donkey's near side.

For every action there is an equal and opposite reaction. If one part of the body is out of balance, another part of the body will compensate, resulting in uneven wear and tear on joints, ligaments and tendons, and muscular asymmetry. The imbalance may be obvious or subtle. Regardless of whether a donkey is to be ridden, driven or competed in-hand, poor balance will have a detrimental effect on his posture both in the short and long term and

will be of greater significance as the donkey ages.

Poor balance can also have an impact on day-to-day handling as tension in the body may create sensitivity to contact and concern when the donkey is approached from his stiffer side. Balance will also affect the ease with which a donkey can stand on three legs when having his feet picked out or his hooves trimmed, and is linked to spatial awareness and proprioception, which affect his ability to walk over different surfaces, through narrow spaces and past unfamiliar objects, and to lead, load, travel, and so on.

Any bracing that occurs through the neck can inhibit, as well as trigger, forward movement. If constant pressure is applied to a donkey's head, the opposition reflex will be engaged and the donkey will either pull back, lean into the headcollar or bridle and increase his speed, or plant.

Many donkeys are taught to stop and move purely from a signal on their head and this can create uneven tension through the body. Teaching a donkey how to organize his whole body and change his centre of gravity when necessary through simple exercises that encourage him to engage his core muscles, lift his back and engage his hindquarters will have many benefits. He will move more freely, have better balance, process new sights and sounds more easily and become lighter in the hand whether he is being led, driven or ridden.

Some donkeys that are driven or ridden may become sensitive to contact on the chest if they are moving consistently on the forehand, lack core strength and struggle with hind limb engagement. Simple body-work techniques and movement exercises in-hand, combined with greater awareness on behalf of the handler, can help the donkey use his body more effectively, thus minimizing fatigue and ensuring he is truly happy in his work.

Proprioception is the part of the nervous system that gives the donkey information with regard to body position. It is also part of the donkey's coordination system. Proprioceptors are primarily located in muscles, tendons and joints. Proprioception is affected by growth spurts, injury and disease and can be improved through simple exercises that increase good body awareness and balance.

Natural balance will vary from donkey to donkey depending on conformation but can also be influenced by many factors, including growth patterns, teeth and foot care, muscle

development, any equipment that may be used when leading or handling the donkey, training and of course any ridden work.

The donkey uses his body for balance but also relies on his eyes (visual balance) and inner ear (vestibular balance) for stability and positional awareness. As the eyes and the ears can be affected by restriction in the upper part of the neck, muscle tension around the cervical vertebrae can have a dramatic effect on the donkey's ability to establish true self-carriage. This tension pattern can be inadvertently triggered by the way the donkey is led, driven and ridden, and this can affect the way he moves and is able to process new sights and sounds.

BODY LANGUAGE AND NERVOUS SYSTEM RESPONSES

It is important to pay attention to all nervous system responses, including heart rate and respiration, the set of the ears, the position of the neck, the appearance of the eye, the

Swishing of the tail, ear flapping and poking the nose forwards can be an obvious sign that something has raised a donkey's suspicion.

shape of the nostril, swishing of the tail and so on. The nervous system never lies. Look out for small, subtle changes, such as tightening of the chin and muzzle, widening of the eye, narrowing of the nostrils, increased respiration rate and so on, as well as more obvious signs of increasing stress and arousal such as stillness or fast movement, shaking the head, ear flapping, pawing the ground, swishing the tail and so on.

The more you look, the more you will see and you will be able to adapt the way you handle or interact with your donkey or change your plans if your donkey is over-faced by what you are asking him to do.

CONFORMATION

In a nutshell, conformation refers to the structural skeletal formation of an animal. Poor conformation – such as skull that is too large, a ewe neck, a long weak back, cow hocks, or disproportional bone length that affects the angle of the joints and so on – will create uneven stress on one or more body parts and result in poor balance. This will affect the ability of the body to function effortlessly both while standing and in motion, and will create excessive wear and tear on the joints, ligaments and tendons, giving rise to stress-related injuries and the early onset of skeletal conditions such as arthritis.

A donkey that is croup high, for example (where the rump is higher than the withers), will have a tendency to brace behind the shoulders through the neck and back, and move with his head high or at speed in order to stay in balance as best he can. A donkey with this conformation fault may also find it hard to stand quietly for the farrier or when tied.

Donkeys tend to internalize stress so outward signs that they are uncomfortable through the body may not always be apparent. Many equines considered to be sour are in fact sore,

and if a donkey has poor conformation, he may be sensitive to contact through the body, difficult to handle, inconsistent in performance, and reluctant to be caught or engage in learning activities; as a result, he will unfairly be labelled as stubborn, difficult or aggressive. In our experience, poor conformation and physical discomfort are the primary causes of unwanted behaviours in animals.

THE COAT AND SKIN

As a desert dweller, the donkey does not produce the grease that makes a horse's coat waterproof. A donkey living in a damp climate must be protected from the rain, either through rugging up when turned out during wet weather or through the provision of appropriate shelter. Some donkeys do not mind getting soaked and will happily stand outside their shelter in the rain, but constantly wet skin may affect their health and well-being, particularly if they are already below par, and may give rise to rain scald, respiratory infections and other health concerns.

Donkeys that have unpigmented skin can be particularly susceptible to sunburn and during warmer weather will probably need to wear a full mesh fly mask and sunscreen to protect sensitive muzzles and ears (or indeed any parts of the body where the skin may be exposed through loss of coat for whatever reason). The ingestion of certain toxic plants can also increase photosensitivity owing to the impact of such plants on the liver.

If adequate shelter is available and temperatures do not drop too low, it isn't necessary to rug your donkey in winter unless he is elderly or unwell. It is worth accustoming your donkey to wearing a rug, however, as some may appreciate the relief a summer sheet can bring when flies and midges are biting. A rugged-up donkey can be an alarming sight to his companion, so it is worth introducing

Sunburn can be a common problem for donkeys with unpigmented skin.

A full flymask will protect sensitive faces and ears from the sun and flies.

anything novel step by step and monitoring the responses of all the donkeys in the social group, as well as the donkey wearing the rug.

As the anatomy of a horse is different from that of a donkey, pony-sized rugs are often too big around the neck. It is therefore worth investing in a rug specifically designed for donkeys if rugs are necessary.

Rolling is an important part of a donkey's life and if they do not have ready access to a sand or dust bath, they will create a dedicated area in the pasture in which to roll.

Unlike horses, donkeys shed their winter coat in the early summer rather than in the spring but many donkeys will hold on to their coat until July. They may look rather moth-eaten as they start to lose their protective winter coat, and of course rough play with donkey friends and plucking by crows looking to line their nests with donkey hair can make the coat look rather patchy through the prolonged shedding period until the sleek, shorter summer coat comes through.

A patchy coat is not always indicative of a health issue but lice can be a common problem, and a frustrating one for both the donkey and the owner. They are more common now than ever before, probably due in part to changes in the use of pesticides. Not all donkeys will itch when they have lice, so regular checks are

Rolling is an important part of a donkey's life and they enjoy the chance to roll in dirt as well as dust.

A patchy coat is common during the spring and summer.

important to ensure that the health and well-being of your donkey is not compromised in any way. Small-toothed combs can remove lice easily, giving you the opportunity to check for their presence, and incorporating the use of such a comb into your grooming routine will ensure that you are aware of lice before the donkey becomes infested. Pay particular attention to the mane, base of the tail, neck and behind the elbows. Groom the whole body gently with the small-toothed comb and wipe the teeth on a white tissue or similar after every couple of strokes. If lice are present, you should see them moving on the paper.

Donkeys that have grazed with livestock or other donkeys and horses may be more susceptible to lice if their companions were never treated for parasites. They may not have been discovered by a previous owner if you have bought or rescued your donkey, so a thorough check is advised even if there are no obvious signs that your donkey is suffering. If you discover that your donkey does have lice, appropriate treatment under veterinary supervision will be required. If your donkey is itchy or has scabs on the skin, it does not necessarily mean that he has lice; it can be a sign that he needs worming, has been scratching and damaged his skin (which may well have become infected), has been bitten by his companion, is irritated by biting flies or midges, or is simply starting to change his coat. Keep an eye on him, and ask your vet to check him over to ensure that he does not require treatment.

Tail rubbing can be a sign of parasitic problems, including lice and worms, but it can also be triggered by insect bites or other skin conditions that affect the skin along the belly, around the sheath or udder, or under the tail. As these areas are hard to reach, affected donkeys may rub their tail and roll more frequently than their companions in an attempt to relieve the irritation.

Most donkeys enjoy a good scratch from time to time, particularly when their winter coat is being shed. The provision of a safe scratching place can help reduce the risk of injury from rubbing itchy necks, flanks and hindquarters on wooden structures that might splinter and further irritate the skin.

Despite the arid origins of his ancestors, a donkey's coat should not feel overly coarse to the touch. An excessively rough coat is likely to be indicative of inappropriate management, including poor nutrition or ill-health, although the texture of the coat varies from breed to breed. A donkey that is well cared for, regularly groomed and on the correct diet will generally have a shiny coat that is soft or relatively soft to the touch.

The coat and skin combined are the largest sensory organs. Donkeys have thicker skin than horses do. The outer layer of the skin forms the largest piece of connective tissue, yet this is an area that is often overlooked when trying to establish where an animal may be holding tension, and one that is often ignored in terms of influencing behaviour and well-being.

Rough grooming, hurried handling and

Raised hair can be linked to sensitive skin, which can result from rough play or from changes to the soft tissue or skeleton.

patting can be overly stimulating for the nervous system and can trigger more arousal, and even concern, particularly if the donkey has any areas of sensitivity in the body. The donkey may fidget when groomed, bite when handled and be reluctant to be caught. While unwanted behaviours can be triggered by many causes, tension through the skin should not be overlooked as it can give you a great deal of information about the donkeys in your care.

Tension in the skin can be addressed through more diligent and careful handling and management, and through the body-work exercises given in this book. If the donkey is persistently concerned about contact on any part of his body, a thorough veterinary examination should be carried out.

Quiet, slow handling has many benefits and non-threatening contact is known to stimulate the release of oxytocin. As well as being more far appropriate for donkeys, or any animal for that matter, mindful contact can help us to become more aware of any tension and temperature changes that may be present.

It is well worth teaching your donkeys that contact on the body is nothing to fear and to accustom them to being touched gently on every part of the body, including the sheath or udder, in and around the mouth, the inside hind limbs and so on. Donkeys love being groomed provided the interaction is comfortable for them. If they are difficult to handle, it is probably because they have areas on the body where contact causes concern. A donkey that has been working on the forehand or is croup high, for example, may be sensitive to contact around the chest, around the girth line, through the back and down the hindquarters. A donkey that is persistently sensitive to contact around the ears may have dental problems or be carrying tension in the upper part of the neck.

Although it may not be easy for the untrained eye to notice changes in gait, muscle development and balance, the skin and coat give very clear visual guides to aid you in the assessment of your donkey and pinpoint any areas that require closer attention. As donkeys tend to shut down and internalize their discomfort, it can be difficult to determine if a donkey is in pain. Being aware of any coat changes through the body and/or down the limbs can alert you to potential causes for your donkey to be reluctant to engage in social activities or contact.

Many timid animals have cold extremities. The lower legs, ear tips and hindquarters may feel cooler to the touch. Cold areas through the body may also be linked to chronic physical problems. Heat can be indicative of a more acute condition that may have arisen as the result of rough play, ill-fitting equipment or damage to the soft tissue and/or skeleton. Some donkeys have a mix of cooler and hotter areas, which may be due to external factors and may vary depending on activity levels and weather conditions, but consistent temperature changes through the body should be noted and investigated if necessary.

Skin receptors make up part of the sensory system and process pressure, vibrational touch, heat, cold, pain, and so on. We can utilize this wonderful part of the anatomy to give the

nervous system new experiences by varying our hand contact, the type of TTouch we may use (lifts, slides, circles or vibrational TTouches) and by introducing different textures such as soft rubber groomers, warming heat pads, sheepskin mitts, and so on. This can be of particular value for nervous donkeys that may be overwhelmed in the big wide world as it offers the opportunity to work with them in a place where they feel safe, such as in the stable or in the paddock, while drip-feeding new information into the sensory system.

The coat can give you a great deal of information about the donkey's general health, his stress levels, his mobility and any changes to the soft tissue and skeleton that might have occurred, as the coat will often change direction where there is tension in the skin. In all cases where significant coat changes were present in a variety of animals that had handling issues, and where a veterinary investigation was carried out, changes to the skeleton and soft tissues were discovered including arthritis and tears in the muscle fibres.

Observing any coat changes through the body can enable owners to see how the work that they are doing with their donkey is having a positive effect as the coat improves, or highlight the need to alter the way they manage and interact with their donkey. Unwanted coat changes that persist or suddenly appear may require veterinary support.

Knowing a little about the importance of the donkey's largest sensory organ helps you to understand why tension in the skin has a direct correlation with the appearance and texture of the hair. Aside from the profound effect that body-work can have on all aspects of the nervous system, the body TTouches can have an almost instantaneous and positive influence on the coat due to their ability to improve circulation and release tension. Dull coats can become shiny in front of your eyes, and dead hair can be shed.

4 Accountability

It can be helpful to think about a donkey's well-being in terms of a bank account. This can enable guardians and carers to identify experiences that are rewarding for the donkey and advance their education, and highlight what might be causing the donkey concern or impacting on his ability to learn.

Genetics, physical health and well-being, along with early experiences, form the basis of the account. Some donkeys will have good investments already in place. They may have inherited a healthy account from their parents, and humans that were a part of their early life will have taken the time to make regular deposits as the youngster began to grow.

Other donkeys may be less fortunate. They have few reserves in place on which to draw and some people will unwittingly, or through choice, take on donkeys that are starting out with a nil balance or an almost empty account. Some donkeys may even have inherited an overdraft owing to the ill-health

'Deposits' can be made by enriching paddocks and barns with games that extend feeding time and offer the donkey the opportunity to use his nose and his brain.

or poor conformation of their parents and their accounts may have been drained further due to a lack of deposits in their formative years.

DEPOSITS

Deposits in the donkey's account are made through positive experiences. They include anything that enables the donkey to succeed and feel great, or adds value to his life. A deposit may be made through the provision of a yummy treat, a scratch or verbal praise; being groomed (provided grooming is a pleasurable experience); a wholesome diet; good physical, mental and emotional well-being; rewarding education that enables him to develop good life skills and grow in confidence; positive interactions with people and other animals; respectful handling; a happy, stress-free environment; appropriate management, and so on.

WITHDRAWALS

Withdrawals are made through negative experiences. They include anything that depletes the donkey's account. This may be poor physical health; forceful handling that deliberately or inadvertently frightens or hurts the donkey; situations that trigger fear; accidents; ill-fitting tack or rugs; unforeseen unfortunate events; frustration; stress; inappropriate diet; a visit from the vet or farrier if either causes the donkey concern; the wrong environment; isolation; poor husbandry, and so on.

INTEREST

Every deposit or withdrawal has the ability to gain interest. Interest can be a bonus that will increase the overall value of all the deposits being made. If a donkey has an overdraft, however, interest will equally apply to any further withdrawals that occur. What we may consider to be a relatively insignificant deposit or withdrawal may therefore have more significance for the overall balance of the donkey's account than we might initially have thought. The greater the combined value of the deposits or withdrawals, the greater the interest accrued.

A donkey that is labelled as aggressive or sour is usually one whose account is desperately overdrawn. For such a donkey, many, many deposits must be made if there is to be any hope of turning the deficit around. A few deposits here and there will not be enough to compensate for the interest on the losses that are mounting up.

Some guardians may be committed to making regular deposits if they have a specific goal in mind, such as preparing a donkey to be ridden, but unless they remember to make continued small investments throughout a donkey's life, and are mindful of any withdrawals that may increase as the animal ages, due to changes in well-being for example, or as a result of an unpleasant experience, the initial growth in the account may not be sustained or sufficient to support that donkey in the long term.

OUR ROLE AS BANKER, MANAGER AND ADVISER

A well-managed bank account provides security. In order to maintain a healthy account for our equine friends, we need to be mindful of our roles whether we are banker, manager or adviser. It is inevitable that there will be some withdrawals from time to time, but if there are more deposits than withdrawals, the occasional withdrawal should not have a long-term detrimental impact on the donkey's account.

We may have sole charge of the account if

we live alone with our donkeys but we may meet others who either add to or deplete our donkey's account along the way. If we work with donkeys, or care for someone else's donkeys on our property, we may become an adviser, or temporary manager for another donkey's account. We may require the services of an additional adviser such as a vet, trainer, farrier or physiotherapist for the donkeys already in our care.

MAKING DEPOSITS AND WITHDRAWALS

Deposits do not only occur when we make a conscious decision to teach a donkey specific life skills using positive reward-based methods. Every interaction we have with a donkey can affect their savings either way. Paying attention to detail and increasing our awareness of all the opportunities that we have to make small deposits throughout the day will bring many rich rewards. We may be amazed at how much can be accumulated in a donkey's account without the need to set aside dedicated banking time.

One simple way to ensure that many deposits are made on a regular basis is to establish where a donkey enjoys being touched and how he responds to being handled by people that he already knows. If we consistently touch him in an area where he is sensitive to contact, or trigger anxiety or bracing through vigorous

Allowing the donkey time to process new sights, sounds and smells without being rushed will help to further his education and develop trust in you.

handling or patting, a withdrawal will be made. This doesn't mean that we should permanently avoid touching a donkey that is sensitive to contact, but we must ensure that we make far more deposits than withdrawals by working on a part of the body that helps the donkey feel safe as we begin to address the reasons why some contact might cause concern.

When leading your donkeys around your property, or interacting with them in the pasture or in their stables, note whether deposits or withdrawals are being made. Do they enjoy being groomed and handled or do they try to move away? Do they walk calmly in balance on a loose line and look around, or do they rush or freeze due to concern? Do they graze contentedly in the paddock or do they fence walk and constantly bray? Think about ways you can help every interaction to be as positive as possible. Slow down your handling and enjoy connecting with your donkey if he is worried by contact on his body. Try stroking or scratching him gently rather than patting him, and if he wants to stop and look at something in the environment as you lead him, let him.

Avoid rushing through these wonderful opportunities and remember to give the donkey plenty of breaks if you are helping him overcome concerns. As with any banking, we need to ensure that the necessary information is in place to avoid the deposit going astray, and we must allow time to let even the smallest investments grow. Give the donkey plenty of opportunities to review his bank statement and to process all the wonderful deposits that have been made.

Prepare in advance for potential withdrawals that may be made by a visit from the vet or farrier, treatment for eye infections, injuries, hoof trimming, travelling, microchipping, injections, bathing and so on by teaching your donkey that contact around his eyes, and around and on his ears, neck, feet, hooves and over every inch of his body is rewarding and something that increases, rather than compromises, the security of his account. Teach in-hand exercises that will help him load and travel calmly without any duress and help him learn that balancing on three legs during feet trimming is nothing to fear. If the unexpected happens or preparation has not been possible, use TTouch techniques to make deposits before, during and/or after any necessary veterinary procedures have been carried out.

Regardless of whether we are working with our own donkeys, or helping to establish a robust account for a client donkey, achievable targets, consistency and patience are the keys. Sustainable financial growth takes time and requires diligent management along the way. It is impossible to make accurate forecasts but if we remember to take care of the pennies, we create potential for the pounds to take care of themselves.

PART 2

5 Know your Donkey

In general, a contented, well-educated donkey is pretty straightforward to handle and manage. Even if you have lived with your donkey for many years and actively engage with him every day, taking time to step back and simply observe him, feel through his body for areas of sensitivity, blocked awareness or tension, and listen to his footfall or any other sounds he might make, such as gulping, can help you to understand him on a whole new level.

In all likelihood, you are probably already aware of your donkey's little habits, such as tilting or turning his head away when you approach with the headcollar, moving around you to place you on his near side if you try to lead him from the right, or insisting on being the first to be groomed/to eat/to walk through the gate or leave the stable, and so on. These behaviours may be viewed as an acceptable part of your donkey's character as they do not create real problems in daily life, but as you start exploring the mobility of his body, including his skin, you may discover that some of these traits, however insignificant, are linked to areas of tension or blocked awareness, and they will begin to diminish or disappear as his overall balance improves.

Knowing exactly where you are starting from will allow you to tailor the suggestions in this book to help each individual donkey. It will also show you how to be more aware of

Turning the head can be a sign that the donkey is processing or disengaging from the activity or interaction. If you note this behaviour when you approach or handle your donkey, pause for a moment and wait until he is able to engage and participate once more.

how behaviours and responses to contact are connected, when his posture improves, and when he might be in need of some additional support.

If you are not accustomed to studying your donkey's habitual movements and posture, start by noting some more obvious habits, such as the appearance of his ears, or the way he organizes his legs and the position of his neck when he is at rest. Remember that nothing in nature is symmetrical and even young donkeys are likely to have areas of tension and an uneven posture due to rough play, as well as natural growth rates and development.

Don't be disheartened if small details do not jump out at you straight away. Keep looking and start making notes. Like all aspects of equine care, improving observational skills requires practice and some people are naturally more adept at using their eyes than others, as learning styles vary from person to person. If you are more of a kinaesthetic (physical) learner, you may find it easier to start with the handling assessments and then re-visit the visual observations to see how they marry up.

Some people find it helpful to take photographs, or slow-motion video, to study at leisure free from other distractions. High-quality digital photography can be invaluable as the images can be easily enlarged to show more detail, but if you do use a picture to glean more information about your donkey friend, bear in mind it only illustrates one moment in time and may not be a true reflection of your donkey's postural habits.

Regardless of the tools you use to help you expand your knowledge, stay open-minded and observe your donkey in different situations, including in the pasture and in his stable, when he is being led, when on the move at liberty and when

If you have the luxury of observing foals, note if they habitually feed from one side more than the other.

dozing in the sun. Avoid jumping to conclusions and look for a pattern over time rather than forming an opinion based on one observation. Becoming a donkey detective can be a truly fascinating and illuminating experience, and further deepen an already well-established bond.

GENERAL OBSERVATIONS

If you don't already do so, pay attention to the bedding if your donkey is stabled overnight or during the day. If a donkey is unsettled, you may see clear tracks, often in a clockwise circular direction, that might suggest at least one of the donkeys has been box-walking. A general mess may well be indicative of a donkey game but can also be a sign of boredom or frustration.

Note how your donkey responds when you approach him with a headcollar. Does he step forward and thrust his nose into the noseband or does he hang back and slightly turn his head away? Do you have to follow him round the stable, yard or field or does he readily walk

Rugs will often slip to the lower side of the pelvis or back if the donkey is unbalanced.

Note the collection of flies around the right eye. Flies will often congregate where there is more stagnation in the body or more fluid in one nostril or one eye, as well as around an injury site.

towards you? Once the headcollar is on, does he march off or does he wait for you to give him a cue? If you ride or drive him, watch his facial expressions when you approach him with the bridle, saddle, breast collar, and so on, and observe his body language as you tack him up. Note if his demeanour changes in any way during work, or when he is being untacked.

Watch your donkey rolling. Does he generally start to roll on the same side each time? Does he roll right over or does he get up and then drop to roll on the other side? If you don't actually see him rolling, look at his coat for mud, dust or bedding. Is there more mud or bedding on one side than the other that might indicate that he lies or rolls more frequently on one side than the other? Is this a common pattern or does it vary?

If your donkey wears a rug or fly sheet, does it continually slip to one side? Rugs will tend to slip to the donkey's lower side if he has uneven muscling and an unlevel posture. If he is bothered by flies, note where they land. You may see that they congregate around one eye more than the other, or hover around a specific area on the body.

Every time you interact with him look for any nervous system responses, such as the tightening of his chin and lips, wrinkling of the nose or eyelids, changes in the position of his ears, hardening or narrowing of the eyes, lifting or dropping the head, turning the head to bite the air (or you), stepping away, an increase in the rate of respiration, and so on. If he ever seems unsettled, consider what might have happened before the behaviour started, as well as what was happening at the time he showed concern.

Feel the weight and mobility of each leg as you clean out his hooves. Do you have to lift his legs in a specific pattern or will he easily pick up any foot in any order when asked? Pay attention to the way he organizes his body as you quietly raise each limb and see if he struggles when you support a particular hoof.

Make a note of the speed with which he exits the stable or comes in from the field, whether this varies from day to day, or changes if you lead him from his left side or his right, or if the ground is sloping or uneven. Is he happy with the farrier, equine dentist and the vet? Does he clamp his jaw when you bridle him or administer a paste wormer, or is he happy for you to handle him around his mouth?

Make as many observations as possible during the day-to-day handling of your donkey and jot them down if necessary, regardless of how irrelevant they may seem.

POSTURAL OBSERVATIONS

Start by looking at the general posture of your donkey at rest and on the move. Avoid staring at him, and keep your eyes soft so that you do not inadvertently alarm him by approaching or watching him with a fixed look. Keep your movements calm and natural if you walk around him or towards him and remember to breathe normally. You will see more if you are relaxed and casually observe rather than watch with great intent. If possible, vary the time of day that you hang out with your donkey as temperature changes through the body, degrees of stiffness, sensitivity to contact and so on may fluctuate depending on different factors.

When you observe him from the front, does he hold his head more to one side than the other? Can you see more of his neck and/ or barrel on the left side or the right? Are his front legs relatively straight or are either of the hooves turned in or out? Are the limbs parallel or does he place one out to the side? When he walks towards you, does he plait (rope walk), or is the movement of his fore limbs reasonably straight?

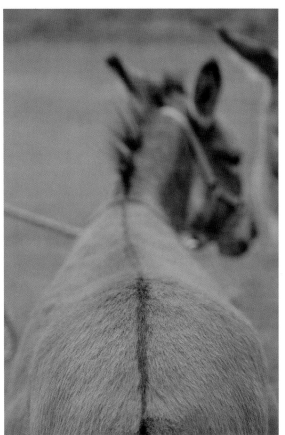

Note the difference between the left and right side of the pelvis and the angle of the dorsal stripe at the base of the tail.

This little donkey in the care of RSPCA Lockwood has arthritis which has affected the mobility through her hindquarters, causing her to rope walk (plait) with her hind limbs.

The greatest learning often derives from doing less; observing grazing patterns when your donkeys are out at pasture can help give you greater understanding of your four-legged friends.

When you observe him from the side, does he look croup high? Is his back dropped or is it level? When at rest does he stand in balance or does he regularly place one leg further forward or back? Remember to look at him from both sides.

Stand behind him if you can and look at the shape of his rump. Is one side more angular than the other? Does he hold his tail slightly to one side or is it straight? How does he position his hind legs? If he is small, or is quite happy for you to stand behind him on a mount block, look along his back and note the slope of his shoulders and the angle of his neck. Is his back evenly developed or does it look lower on one side? Does one shoulder appear higher than the other?

When your donkey is out in the field, note his grazing pattern. Does he move his neck more to the left than the right as he pulls the grass? Does he consistently place a particular foreleg further forward than the other? Does his lower jaw move evenly in both a clockwise and anti-clockwise direction or does he habitually favour grinding the grass one way?

Note the differences in the shape, height and appearance of this donkey's nostrils and muzzle from left to right. His mother has the same pattern.

More detailed observations

When looking at your donkey head on, note whether the ears are level. Does one appear to be higher or further forward than the other? Do both ears move freely when the donkey is processing information or communicating, or is the movement consistently more restricted in one ear than the other regardless of the direction or proximity of the stimulus that may have got his attention? Is the space between the ears and the poll relatively even on both sides or does one ear look closer to this bony projection than the other?

Does one eye appear to be higher than the

Changes in the balance of the fore limbs and tension in the neck can create a head tilt. It may be subtle or more obvious, and is often accompanied by unlevel ears.

other? Are his eyes a similar size or does one eye look smaller or more almond-shaped than the other? Can you see more of the eye on one side than the other when you are looking at him from the front? Are his nostrils even or does he habitually wrinkle his muzzle on one side? Can you see more of the lower lip on one side? Are his whiskers shorter on one side or do they grow at a different angle to the whiskers on the other side? Can you see the same amount of cheek on both sides?

Start looking at the coat, taking into account any natural swirls or areas where the coat may be shedding or ruffled following a game. If your donkey has a dorsal stripe, note whether it is reasonably straight or crooked; a crooked dorsal stripe can be a really good guide to the development of the donkey's top line and overall balance. Bear in mind that some donkeys have a naturally wavy dorsal stripe, however, so use your hands to establish if there are any corresponding areas of touch sensitivity or irregular muscle development through the back. Look at the hair at the top of the tail. Is it relatively straight or does it all lie to the right or left?

Study the hair on his shoulders and chest. Does the hair look roughly symmetrical on both sides of his body or does it appear straighter or change direction on a particular side? Observe the pattern, colour and texture of the coat all over his body and if you notice an area where the coat stands up or changes direction, does this correspond to any areas of blocked awareness or sensitivity that you discovered when you touched him with your hands? The colour, direction and texture of the hair changes where damage has occurred or where tension has been present for some time.

Look for dark patches on a lighter donkey, light areas on a darker donkey and of course the presence of white hairs that might correspond to areas where the donkey is reactive to contact. Some donkeys have natural shading and different coloured markings but if an area

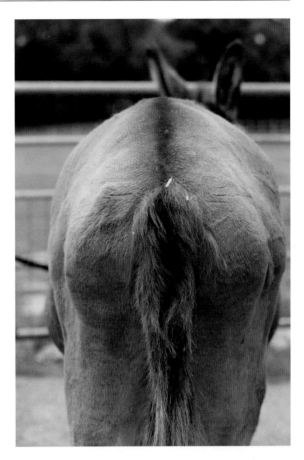

The hair and the position of the tail will often mirror the balance of the donkey's back. Here the hair at the top of the tail moves off to the right.

of light or dark is more prevalent on one part of the body, or suddenly appears, it may be indicative of soft tissue or skeletal change.

LISTEN

If your donkey is on firm ground, listen to his footfall as he walks. You may notice that one hoof lands more heavily as he moves, or that he scuffs the surface with one or more of his toes. If leading your donkey over poles, pay attention to which toe (or toes) clips the poles. Does this vary or is it the same foot (or feet) every time?

Listen to any sounds your donkey might

make, such as gulping, heavy breathing, and so on, and if your donkey is usually expressive in terms of braying when you approach or if he is anticipating his feed, note if he becomes abnormally quiet.

FLAT HAND EXPLORATION

If your donkey enjoys being touched, you can learn more about his posture by stroking him gently all over his body with one hand. Hold the lead rope with the other hand, or rest it on your donkey if he is at liberty to maintain a supportive connection. If you do put two hands

on your donkey, pay attention to the position of both hands to ascertain which hand triggered a reaction, if any.

Stand slightly to one side and start at your donkey's head if he is used to you handling him around his face. Stroke his face, cheeks, under the jaw and around the muzzle. Break it down into micro-sessions by slowly stroking him no more than three or four times before quietly taking your hand away. Watch his reactions as you stroke him, but also when you pause. We can sometimes learn more about how an animal feels about our interactions when we stop and give them the opportunity to respond.

Observe the natural position of your donkey's head and neck when he is at rest and remember to take the weather and the angle of the ground into account when checking balance, tension or temperature changes through the body.

Watching the position of the donkey's ears can indicate which side of his body he is focusing on. If you use two hands to make contact, experiment by using one at a time if you notice a response.

Continue down his neck, around his chest, between his front legs, along his back and down the ribs, remembering to pause every few strokes. Pay attention to any warmer or cooler areas or places where the coat may feel rough. Stroke him gently over his hindquarters and down his tail. Stroke him around the girth area and all over his belly. Make a mental note if you feel any variations in temperature, and check again at a later date. Take the weather and time of day into account as your donkey may have been resting in the sun or standing in cool shade.

Feel the contours of his whole body and, if it is safe to do so, run your hand gently down each leg. If you know he is worried about having his legs touched, skip this part of the assessment process for now.

Remember to switch sides and see if you can feel any disparity from left to right in muscle tone, temperature or the quality of his coat. Remember to observe his nervous system responses; some donkeys react completely differently when touched or handled from the opposite side.

If your donkey is shy or easily worried, start on his shoulder or neck and use the back of your hand. Many animals that lack confidence

Donkeys often have quite specific play or grooming behaviours and may have more lumps or bumps on one part of their body as a result.

become anxious when touched on the head, and find contact with the back of the fingers or hand less threatening than being stroked with the palm of the hand. An anxious donkey may also prefer you not to touch him simultaneously with both hands and to stay away from his legs and hindquarters until his confidence develops.

Don't rush through this process. Enjoy connecting with him and remember you are working with him, not doing something to him. Keep the movements slow and rhythmical. You are 'reading' him with your hand and if you hurry you will speed-read and might miss some important details of his story. If he moves away at any point, go back to touching him in an area where contact was acceptable and make a note of where he showed concern.

If you find areas that trigger a response, don't worry. Start implementing some of the suggestions in this book and monitor the effect they have. Remember that animals, just like humans, have a more dominant side, suffer from occasional stiffness and blocked awareness through the body, load one or more parts of their body unevenly, occasionally slip or fall, and can suffer the effects of a boisterous game.

Many postural irregularities can be easily addressed with greater knowledge and awareness but if you do consistently find an area that triggers changes in your donkey's response to contact and it does not improve over time (or worsens), ask your vet to carry out a thorough health check. If any physical problems are found that need additional support in conjunction with appropriate veterinary care, discuss what options might be best. We regularly enlist the services of vets and other therapists with the vet's consent who offer acupuncture, physiotherapy, McTimoney chiropractics, osteopathy and so on to support the work that we already do.

The exercises shared in this book combine well with other modalities and provide tools to improve the health and well-being of our donkey friends, but they should never be used as a replacement for appropriate veterinary care.

6 The Tellington TTouch and Connected Riding

THE TELLINGTON TTOUCH

The Tellington TTouch was developed in the USA by Linda Tellington Jones over forty years ago. It has its roots in the Feldenkrais Method, a form of integrated body-work and gentle exercises, that improves posture, movement and well-being in humans. Linda, a highly experienced and successful horsewoman, initially intended to study the Feldenkrais Method to enhance the athletic ability of her riding students and in the 1970s she enrolled in a four-year certification training course at the Humanistic Psychology Institute in San Francisco taught by the renowned Israeli physicist Moshe Feldenkrais. Within a week of beginning the course, however, Linda recognized the remarkable potential this approach might have for equines.

Linda was already using massage techniques that she had learned from her grandfather Will Caywood on her competition horses with great success. She co-authored *Massage and Physical Therapy for the Athletic Horse* in 1965 with her first husband Wentworth Tellington, but after meeting Feldenkrais her interest shifted from working purely with the muscles of equines to influencing their nervous system as a whole. After thirty-three years of working with horses, Linda felt that she was seeing horses with new eyes.

Linda's sister, Robyn Hood, was influential in establishing TTouch as a technique that could be easily taught. It is a logical, forward-thinking approach to the training, handling and rehabilitation of all animals, and is now used widely around the world by those who work or share their lives with animals, including vets, veterinary nurses, trainers, riders, animal handlers, those working for welfare organizations, behaviour counsellors, physical therapists and animal guardians.

The gentle, non-invasive body-work movements known as TTouches, on and with the animal's body, increase awareness, release tension, improve circulation, lower heart rate and respiration, and reduce stress. They give animal guardians and care givers positive ways of influencing the nervous system, enabling animals to learn and move beyond their instinctive and often fear-based responses. The calm, slow, ground-work exercises, leading equines through patterns of poles, over different surfaces, raised boards and the low-level see-saw, help to improve posture, proprioception, self-carriage and self-control.

The Tellington TTouch approach recognizes an inextricable link between posture and behaviour and focuses on what the animal *can* achieve. Equines that are exposed to TTouch show a marked willingness to learn and to participate in human-led activities. They become more social, develop greater self-confidence and self-control, become more consistent in performance and behaviour, and

Teaching a donkey to negotiate obstacles or walk over a low-level see-saw can help improve balance and coordination: two skills required for effortless daily handling and successful stress-free loading and travelling.

CIRCULAR TTOUCHES

Imagine small clock-faces all over your donkey's body. Place your fingers, finger tips or the palm of your hand on your donkey at six, depending on the area on which you are working and the type of TTouch you are using. Keep your hand relaxed and allow your fingers to flex as you work. Move the same piece of tissue all the way around the imaginary clock-face in one and a quarter circles, finishing at eight or nine. The majority of animals seem to prefer clockwise circles but some settle more with anti-clockwise movements.

Starting at six enables you to begin and complete each circle by moving the tissue in an upwards direction, which feels more relaxing. Making one circle instead of one and a quarter makes the movement feel incomplete. Try taking three seconds to complete each TTouch but work a little more quickly if your donkey starts to fidget.

It is important that you do not press your hand or poke your fingers into the donkey's skin but maintain enough contact to be able to move the actual skin rather than sliding your hand over his coat. Experiment with slight variations in pressure until you find the right connection for your donkey.

Pay attention to the quality of each movement and remember to breathe. Pause for a count of one or two seconds after each individual circular TTouch then lightly slide your hand or fingers over your donkey's coat to the next small clock-face and repeat the movement to make connected TTouches. Try random TTouches on different parts on your donkey's head or body if he cannot settle.
Avoid making multiple circles in one place.

are easier to handle in every aspect of daily life.

The Tellington TTouch is not only beneficial for donkeys that have physical or behavioural concerns. It is a highly rewarding way of interacting with all animals, and countless animal guardians around the world use these effective techniques not only to address common problems but to enhance well-being, and as a way of setting up young or uneducated animals for success.

Body-work

The body TTouches break down into three main groups: circles, slides and lifts. They consist of a variety of specific light-pressure touches and strokes. The aim is to increase mind/body awareness, release tension, improve circulation and to give the donkey new information and experiences by engaging the sensory aspect of the nervous system.

The circular TTouches are the foundation of the TTouch technique. The fingers (or hand) actually move the donkey's skin gently in one and a quarter circles.

For the lifts, the hand gently moves and supports the tissue of the body, then slowly releases it to the resting position. This often assists an animal to release muscle tension around a specific joint or body part, and lifts are usually used on legs, shoulders, hindquarters and along the back and neck. They can be combined with the circular TTouches or used on their own.

Slides consist of slow gentle movements, such as ear slides where the ear is stroked from the base right out to the tip, or long, mindful strokes that connect one body part

LIFTS

Use the palm or back of your hand to gently glide your donkey's skin over the underlying structures. Keep the range of movement small and pause as you 'lift' the skin maintaining the contact before you slowly lower your hand to return the skin to its original starting place. Although the movement looks minimal to an observer, the sensation can be quite profound.

to another or on the mane, coat or tail. These reduce stress, reinforce the animal's spatial awareness and release tension. Hair slides can be a useful starting point for some donkeys that are worried by direct hand contact on their body.

In addition to the three main groups of TTouches, vibrational and combination TTouches are also used. The variety of TTouches enables animal carers to introduce many new experiences to the nervous system in a calm non-threatening way and in the safety of an environment that the donkey knows. This is of particular benefit for animals that may be easily overwhelmed by novel situations and cannot adapt easily to change.

The position of the hand and the pressure and type of TTouch used will vary from donkey

SLIDES

Unlike lifts and the majority of the circular TTouches, slides do not focus on moving the skin, although naturally there will be some release of the tissue as you work. Use the palm or back of your hand to make smooth flowing strokes over your donkey's face and body, down his tail and along his ears.

to donkey, and will be dependent on the donkey's responses to contact and the part of the body that is being TTouched. As well as finding contact with the back of the hand or fingers (as in Llama TTouch) far less threatening, nervous and defensive animals may initially only be able to tolerate being TTouched on their chest, neck or shoulder.

The TTouches are largely named after animals that either inspired the particular body-work exercise or as a point of reference to help guardians and care-givers remember the shape and position of the hand and/or the pattern of movement created by each TTouch.

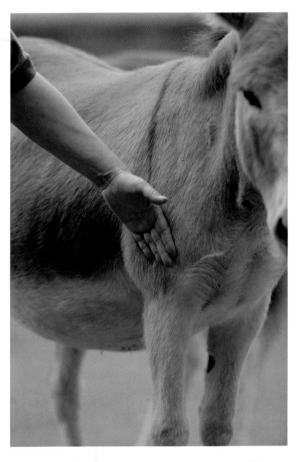

The Llama TTouch was named after the animal that inspired it, as the camelids that experienced this TTouch accepted contact more readily when the back of the hand was used.

GROUND-WORK

Ground-work exercises are an important part of both the Tellington TTouch technique and Connected Riding, and are beneficial for many reasons. Slow movement exercises that encourage flexibility and improve balance are more effective in releasing habitual patterns of bracing than lungeing a donkey or simply walking him in straight lines. They can give the donkey new experiences and teach him to respond rather than merely react to his environment. Engaging slow-twitch muscles can increase dopamine and serotonin, and this approach can offer a vital stepping-stone for fearful animals and those that cannot tolerate contact on the body.

Think of the ground-work exercises as being like yoga or physical therapy for your donkey. They encourage the 'feel-good factor' and help to provide a foundation on which further life skills can be built. They can help donkeys overcome concerns about loading, provide a starting place for driving, riding or competing in-hand, improve movement, build confidence, encourage engagement, teach a donkey to be led and handled from both sides, and so on.

The aim, as with all aspects of TTouch, is to improve balance and body awareness and to help a donkey move beyond his instinctive reactions. Incorporating TTouch ground-work exercises into your regular routine can add variety and fun to the day-to-day handling of your donkey and give you ways of engaging with him even if you do not wish to ride or

Teaching a donkey to negotiate patterns of poles on the ground can improve balance and proprioception, while providing necessary mental stimulation.

drive your friend. Donkeys are highly intelligent and love to learn new skills, and ground-work exercises in-hand can give them appropriate much-needed mental stimulation.

When exercise is reduced due to lack of time, poor weather or for physical reasons, ground-work can be helpful for calming busy donkeys that may be frustrated by a lack of opportunity to engage in other activities. The exercises can also encourage them to become more settled in other aspects of their training as negotiating patterns of poles on the ground, walking over different surfaces and so on helps to improve focus and flexibility in both the mind and the body, and promotes calm.

The ground-work exercises are also beneficial for the handler. They can help improve your own balance, refine your leading techniques, offer you new ways to interact with your donkey while teaching him great life skills, and give you a greater understanding of your four-legged friend.

There isn't any set pattern to the way you can use ground-work and you are limited only by your own imagination. Think about what you would like to achieve and be flexible in your approach. Take every opportunity to praise your donkey with quiet words or a little scratch so he knows that he is on the right track when you are teaching him new skills.

Some donkeys may not benefit from every exercise and you can tailor the ground-work to suit your own goals and needs. Some of the exercises that we have used with great success are listed in this book but the explanations of why we use these techniques are merely intended to give you some idea of the efficacy of the individual exercises and are by no means exhaustive.

CONNECTED RIDING

We have also included some body-work, ridden and ground-work techniques and tips, developed by US horsewoman Peggy Cummings. A passionate horse lover and rider from early childhood, Peggy studied with many clinicians to improve her riding skills throughout her years as a professional horsewoman. As she moved into her forties, she became frustrated with her inability to progress in her riding owing to pain in her back and legs. Decades of more conventional riding had taken its toll on her body.

It is sometimes said that frustration can be the first step to improvement, and this was certainly true for Peggy. To overcome the problems she was having, and in the hope of rediscovering the joy and ease of riding she had experienced as a child, Peggy looked for possibilities and solutions. She studied first with Sally Swift of Centered Riding fame, then with Linda Tellington Jones, and finally with Major Andres Lindgren. Eventually Peggy amalgamated all her new-found knowledge and developed her own system of body-work, ground-work and ridden exercises called Connected Riding to improve posture and movement for both horse and rider.

Peggy's insights and knowledge have contributed to how TTouch is taught today by providing additional, highly effective techniques that help to release habitual patterns of bracing in animals and their guardians.

PART 3

7 Seventy-five Tips and Techniques to Help the Donkeys in Your Care

CONNECTING WITH NOVICE AND NERVOUS DONKEY

The nature versus nurture debate continues in all aspects of animal care and behaviour. Not every donkey that exhibits fear will have been treated poorly, while some donkeys that have been abused still have utmost trust in the human race. Donkeys can be really fearful of being handled due to a variety of reasons. Confidence is inherited to a degree, and the approach is largely going to be the same regardless of whether you are working with a donkey that is naturally timid, or one that has been treated badly, neglected or simply left unhandled.

All donkeys are individual and, although good experiences, appropriate husbandry and rewarding education are crucial for the health and well-being of all equids, the role that genetics can play in terms of behaviour as well as physical attributes cannot be overlooked. Some donkeys need more time to process information, while others seemingly take every new experience in their stride.

All donkeys appreciate simple, calm, consistent and logical steps when learning new skills, but it is important to work in really short sessions when interacting with novice or nervous donkeys so that they do not become overloaded in any way. As their stress levels increase, so their ability to learn and retain information will decrease.

Remember to think about what the donkey may be learning from every new experience and consider how each step in his education can be broken down into its simplest form. Take every opportunity to make multiple deposits in order to balance your donkey's account (*see* Accountability) and be aware that what we may perceive as a pleasant experience may be viewed as a withdrawal by a donkey that has few, if any, positive reserves in place.

1. Containment with two wands

A wand is a long dressage schooling stick. It is an integral part of the Tellington TTouch approach to equine education and is used to improve balance and body awareness when leading the donkey through ground-work exercises. The wand can also be used to initiate contact when working with donkeys that are afraid or unsure of what human contact may mean.

Catching a donkey that is worried about being caught or touched can be extremely challenging. Pinning a donkey in a corner and making a grab for his headcollar will only confirm his concerns, but the use of wands enables you to contain the donkey without trapping him and ultimately to touch him without escalating his distress by crowding him or forcing contact upon him.

Although many nervous donkeys will respond to a quiet approach and food, some fearful donkeys remain highly suspicious and cannot eat when they are anxious. Patience is the key. Although the following process may seem time-consuming, we know from experience that it will save time in the long run, and each step helps to increase trust whilst establishing good foundations on which further learning exercises can be built.

Even though approaching a nervous donkey with two long schooling sticks may be the last thing that you might imagine as being practical or humane, this technique has helped countless equines quickly overcome their fears.

Considerations

Avoid the temptation to rush through the stages. You will be amazed at how fast the donkey learns that human contact is nothing to fear when you work at his pace. Always remember, less is more.

Begin by calmly herding the donkey into a smaller space if he is at liberty in a large field or enlist the help of several friends if you cannot create a safe smaller area in which to work. Be mindful not to chase the donkey, but gently guide him towards a corner of the field or a safe and appropriate enclosure. If the donkey is already in a barn, pen, small paddock or stable, it is imperative that he has the freedom to move around to some extent to prevent him from panicking and becoming defensive if he feels cornered and trapped. Always give him a get-out clause.

If at any point his behaviour escalates, stop. You will have inadvertently pushed him too far.

Think about what you observed in his nervous system responses before his body language became 'louder' and make a note to stop the next session before he has to shout.

Avoid separating him if he has company. If an anxious donkey has a more confident friend, so much the better as you can start by working with his more outgoing companion, but if you are working with two or more nervous donkeys, the same techniques can still be applied. You will generally notice that one of the donkeys develops trust more quickly and, as donkeys learn a lot by observing the behaviour of their social group, you may find that this in itself helps the more timid donkey grow in confidence.

How to

Start by holding a wand in each hand. Think of them as being an extension of your arms and practise moving them fluidly with your left and right hands, both independently and also at the same time, before you approach your donkey. As simple as this may seem, some people find it difficult to be dextrous with their non-dominant hand and slow, controlled, mindful movements with the wands are crucial to keep the donkey calm.

The distance at which you start will depend upon the individual donkey. The aim is to be able to use the wands to contain the donkey but still allow him space to move around prior to using the schooling sticks to initiate contact. Before the donkey can be expected to accept contact with the wands, he needs to be comfortable seeing two long white sticks moving in the air. Add the proximity of a person and there is already a potentially highly stressful situation for the donkey long before contact is even made.

Hang out with your donkey at a distance that is comfortable for him. Take note if he tries to increase the space between you. If he does, and it is possible for you to move away, find a place to stand where your presence causes less concern. If he is in the company of a more confident donkey, he may hide behind his friend. If this is the case, work with the bolder donkey but remember that the more timid donkey will learn less if his anxiety is high.

Stand slightly to the side, soften your posture and remember to breathe. Stay there for a few moments then quietly walk away. Fill water buckets or do other chores then go back and hang out near your donkey once more, starting at the distance that was acceptable. If he remains settled, move a little closer. If he is really worried by the sight of the wands, hold them together in one hand and out of sight by keeping them by your side or behind your back. Casually bring them out for a moment, before hiding them once again.

Work in micro-sessions if your donkey is really worried and gradually build up the steps until you can stand relatively near him with a wand in each hand. Once your donkey is comfortable with you standing in close proximity with static wands, start slowly moving them in the air.

You may need to move one at first and then the other before using them both together. Remember to give him plenty of breaks. Keep the movement soft and fluid rather than waving them wildly back and forth.

Progress until you can stand near, or approach, your donkey with a wand in each hand without triggering high anxiety. Extend your arms outwards at an angle to suggest a boundary. If he panics, move away and slow the process down. You should find that he is confident enough to stay within a smaller area relatively quickly. If you are working with two donkeys, avoid the temptation to rush through this process as you want to minimize the risk of sending the more anxious donkey away and separating him from his friend.

2. Initiating contact with two wands

Although this exercise is similar to 'Introducing a single wand', as described in the body-work section, it can be more beneficial to use two

Create a mobile boundary using your arms and the wands, and gently guide the donkey across the enclosure.

wands when helping a particularly anxious donkey overcome any handling concerns as it helps to diffuse his focus and is a natural progression from the containment exercise with two wands. It also provides a useful stepping-stone for using a catch rope when working with donkeys that cannot be haltered or easily caught.

Considerations

Avoid working too quickly and remember that a quiet donkey may not be feeling calm inside: in fact, he may be shutting down.

How to

Once the donkey is able to stand quietly while you contain him with the wands, you can progress to touching him with them. The majority of timid animals find contact on the chest and down the front of the legs more acceptable than on other parts of their body.

Start by gently moving the wands around the donkey without touching him with them. Remember to pause to give him time to process the sight and sensation of the wands moving near him in the air. When we teach handlers how to work effectively with wands by practising with a human partner, many people report they can feel the presence of the wand before it actually makes contact with their body.

If the donkey turns to sniff and explore either wand, it is likely that he will be more confident when you touch him with the wand than a donkey that is too anxious to initiate contact. Even if he doesn't choose to engage with the wands himself, he will usually settle relatively quickly once he learns that being stroked with the wand is nothing to fear.

Once the donkey is able to stand quietly (without going into freeze) as you gently move the wands in the air, you can progress to touching him with the wands. With one wand, stroke him down his chest and the front of his forelegs, while holding the second wand

Move the wands around the donkey as though you are drawing his outline in the air and gradually decrease the distance between the wands and his body.

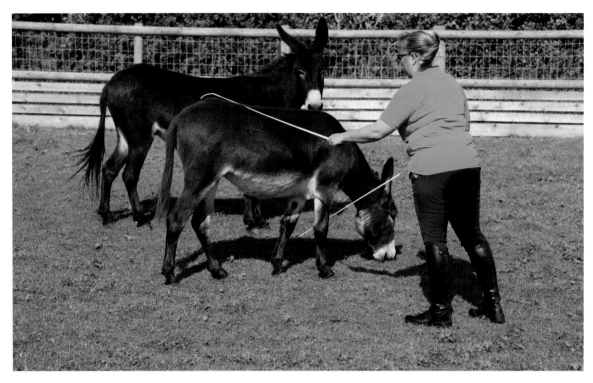

Initiating contact with two wands is both practical and safe as it enables you to touch a donkey without crowding him, and it gives you more opportunities for observation.

out and angled slightly forward to suggest a boundary behind the donkey's rump. If he backs away from the contact, let him and step further to the side to invite him forward once more with a gentle fluid waving motion of the wand behind him. At no point should the wand be used to tap him.

Stroke him down the front legs once more. If he settles, try moving the second wand in the air over his back from his withers to his croup while you maintain a connection on his forequarters with the other wand. Remember to give him plenty of breaks so that he can process every minute step.

Extend the area that you are touching by stroking one wand along the top of his crest from the middle of your donkey's neck to the base. Use the second wand to make a connection along the bottom of his neck.

Progress by stroking him down his front legs with one wand, and along his back with the second. Stroke him gently from his withers to his croup and gradually build up the contact until you can stroke him over the hindquarters and partially down the tail.

Drip-feed more information into the nervous system by using one wand to stroke him down the back of his front legs, then use both wands to stroke the front and back of his forelegs simultaneously, and keep building until you can stroke him down the front of his hind legs while using the other wand to stroke his forelegs.

If you are using the wands to catch the donkey, it is not necessary to continue until you can stroke him over every part of his body but it is well worth teaching him that being stroked is a pleasant experience. Break the sessions down over several days if possible and remember to stroke him along his belly as well as right down to his hooves.

3. Using a catch rope

Many fearful animals are alarmed by contact on and around their extremities, which can lead to problems when trying to catch a nervous donkey in the field. Turning the donkey out in a break-away headcollar offers a safe and practical option as you work on building his trust and confidence but if the donkey indulges in a good scratch on any boundary, the headcollar might fall off.

If something has alarmed the donkey while he was enjoying the freedom of the pasture, or if he is generally worried by contact around his head, he may be reluctant to let you put his headcollar back on even if he is happy to approach you. A light catch rope is an invaluable piece of equipment to have in your tool kit, and it is well worth planning ahead if you share your life with a donkey that might be difficult to catch at times.

Considerations

If you know your donkey can be hard to catch, practise the wand exercises described above as this will save you valuable time and enable you to be more dextrous with the schooling sticks. Remember to work at your donkey's pace and break down this exercise into several small steps to give him time to process what you are asking him to do. It is often during the breaks that most change occurs. As frustrating as an at-liberty donkey can be when you are in a rush, patience is the key.

You can purchase a small light catch rope online from the Tellington TTouch stores, or make your own. Ensure the rope you choose

is soft and light. Heavy abrasive rope will be uncomfortable for your donkey and difficult to handle.

How to

Quietly approach the donkey with two wands and use them to initiate contact. Pause for a moment and repeat to ensure your donkey is comfortable being touched with the wands. Turn the wands around so that you are now using the button ends and stroke him again. You can use the button end to do gentle zigzags along his neck and back. Wrap one end of the catch rope loosely around one wand and stroke the donkey over the top of his neck with the rope and wand. Use the second wand to stroke him along the base of his neck and down the front of his chest if necessary.

Allow the catch rope to slide off the end of the wand so that the end of the rope is resting on the middle of his crest. Keep hold of the line along with the wand. Ensure there is sufficient length of rope so that you can bring the rope around his neck. Stroke the donkey with both wands to help keep him calm and engaged. If he moves away and the rope slides off, quietly repeat the process.

Once the donkey is happy to stand with the rope over the top of his neck, use the wand to scoop up the end of the rope and draw it towards you. If your donkey panics at any point, stop and go back a step. If you have already worked successfully with the wands, the sight of the rope coming away from his neck is less likely to alarm the donkey. Lay the wands on the ground if you cannot manage the wands and rope at the same time.

Pay attention to his nervous system responses and remember that a quiet donkey may be shutting down. If he goes into freeze, remove the rope and let him move before going through the steps once more.

Once the donkey is happy to stand with the

rope around his neck, hold the short length of rope in one hand and the longer length in your other hand. Gently slide the rope back and forth, but avoid rubbing the donkey's neck or moving the line too vigorously. This is to accustom him to the feel of the rope moving on his neck without inciting panic. If he becomes concerned, pause or remove the rope completely and start again.

Encourage him to take a step towards you by giving a gentle ask-and-release signal on the rope. Avoid pulling, as this will trigger the opposition reflex and he will brace against the sensation. Once he is happy to stand and move with the rope around his neck, attach the short end of the rope to the longer length with a

Threading the line through the neck loop from front to back ensures the line will not tighten around the throat area when the rope is popped over the donkey's nose.

Avoid the temptation to rush through the steps if your donkey is happy to stand with the rope around his neck. Use gentle TTouches on his body to help him settle and relax and observe his responses at all times.

quick-release knot. If you are using a TTouch catch rope, attach the clip to the ring. Make sure that the rope cannot tighten around your donkey's neck.

This may be enough to enable you to pop his headcollar on but if he remains worried, slide the loop up his neck, make a small loop in the longer length and feed it through the neck loop from front to back as shown in the photographs. Pop the smaller loop over the donkey's nose to support his head. Put his headcollar on over the rope, attach a lead line and remove the catch rope.

Make sure you lift the rope over the sensitive muzzle and ensure it does not tighten around the nasal bone.

If you do not have a headcollar to hand, twist the rope to make a second loop and quietly place it over the top of the existing loop around his nose. You can then lead your donkey in his new neat temporary halter. Make sure that the loops do not tighten around his sensitive nasal bone.

4. Sliding line

Novice and nervous donkeys may freeze, brace, pull back or rush forward when led. Some may even bolt. Applying pressure on the lead line can create anxiety and trigger the opposition reflex, thus exacerbating the donkey's issues when being led.

Using a sliding rope enables you to quickly remove the line should the donkey tank off and disappear across the pasture if you inadvertently miss his signs of escalating concern, thus minimizing the risk of injury caused by a trailing lead. It also encourages you to move your arms and shoulders, which will help reduce tension on the line.

You can also give subtle signals by sliding the rope through the ring on the headcollar to help soften the donkey through the poll joint and keep him relaxed, yet fully engaged.

Considerations

Avoid wrapping any part of the line around your hand and ensure that you do not have long loops in the rope that could trip you up or get caught around your donkey's legs. Wear gloves if there is any risk that your donkey will shoot forwards or backwards. If he does back up, go with him. Most equines stop moving backwards once tension on the line is released. If he feels a pull on the rope, he may panic.

How to

Use a long length of climbing rope or soft magician's rope. The rope needs to be fairly light and comfortable for you to hold. Thread the line through the ring on the side of your donkey's headcollar. Ensure that the rope does not tilt the hardware into your donkey's face. Take one end of the line in each hand and gently slide the rope back and forth. Pause and note your donkey's responses. Ensure he has enough space to move without being inhibited by the position of your own body. Overcrowding your donkey may encourage him to lean into the line, freeze or pull away.

The sliding line can help to reduce tension on the lead line and enables you to influence the poll joint area instead of inadvertently applying pressure on the headstall.

If he is unsure about walking forward, and is watching the line, take the rope in your nearest hand and use your outside arm to encourage him to walk forward before taking the rope in both hands once more. Refrain from pulling back on the line with your other hand. You can also try stroking the line (as described in the leading exercise) and use voice cues and a gentle slide on the line to encourage him to move, slow down, turn and halt. Practise this exercise from both sides to improve your donkey's balance and to give him a new experience.

5. The Bucket Game

This ingenious game was devised by animal behaviour and training consultant Chirag Patel, who earned his BSc (Hons) in Veterinary Sciences from the Royal Veterinary College, London, and his Postgraduate Certificate in Clinical Animal Behaviour from the University of Lincoln, UK. He also holds an advanced diploma in practical aspects of companion animal behaviour and training from the Centre of Applied Pet Ethology and works with many organizations around the world. His passion is the application of behaviour change science and ethics to improve the life of animals living under human care.

The bucket game has become a valuable addition to our tool kit when working with animals. It allows the donkey to choose when he participates in what he is being asked to do and gives clear visual information to the guardian as to when the donkey starts to struggle and needs a break.

Considerations

Donkeys that are really fearful may not be able to eat. This game is best suited to donkeys that hang back from people in the stable or the field, and those that have specific concerns about being tacked up, caught, handled, groomed, touched on a specific part of their body or treated for injuries.

Introduce the bucket game over a boundary fence or low stable door to prevent the donkey from becoming pushy around the food. When delivering the treat, move your hand towards the donkey's chest to encourage him to step back before taking the food from your hand.

If the game is to be used to help a donkey become more confident about approaching people in the field or enclosure, it is imperative that the game is not 'poisoned' by luring the donkey to the bucket with the promise of food and then taking the opportunity to make a quick grab for his headcollar. Likewise, if this brilliant game is used to help a donkey overcome concerns when handled, all interaction should cease the moment the donkey looks or steps away from the bucket until he is ready to engage once more. Always remember this is a game of choice.

How to

You will need a small bucket that can hold plenty of treats, and is easy for you to carry and hold. You will also need some food. If your donkey is really food motivated you may only need to use small amounts of hay or grass. You can also use slices of carrot cut lengthways, donkey nuts or small pieces of apple. Ensure that any treat you use cannot choke your

Reward the donkey the moment he looks at the bucket and move your hand towards him so he learns to step back before he takes the treat.

Wait for a moment if the donkey sniffs or explores the bucket with his nose.

donkey if he grabs it from your hand and swallows it whole.

Load your bucket and stand next to the boundary fence or stable door. The moment the donkey looks at the bucket, say 'Yes', take out a treat and offer it to him from a flat, open palm, or drop it quietly on the floor or ground if your donkey cannot take it from your hand at first.

Every time your donkey looks at the bucket, say 'Yes', and give him a treat. Avoid keeping your hand in the bucket in anticipation as this will teach your donkey to watch your hand and not engage with the bucket. If your donkey pushes at the bucket with his nose, step back so that he cannot make contact with the bucket.

Work in short sessions. If your donkey steps away, wait for a moment rather than assuming he has tired of the game. He may well be processing and will probably step forward to engage once more.

Build this exercise up on a regular basis and practise both in the stable and out in the field. Once your donkey has learnt that looking at the bucket results in a treat, you can progress. The possibilities are endless but it is perhaps easier to explain how to incorporate the bucket game into the management of a donkey to address a particular concern. Whether you are helping a donkey to overcome concerns about being groomed, having his feet touched and so on, the steps described in the next section, 'Introducing a new person', will be the same.

6. Introducing a new person using the Bucket Game

The majority of donkeys will quickly build trust in a guardian if they find interactions are rewarding, but they may not automatically transfer that same level of trust to someone who is less familiar to them. The bucket game enables you to observe when your donkey is processing the presence of a person close by and when he is ready for contact to be made.

How to

Once your donkey has learned the link between looking at the bucket and receiving a reward, ask the person you wish to introduce to him to stand a little distance from you. If your donkey is watching the person, wait. The moment he looks back at the bucket, say 'Yes', and give him a treat. If he cannot engage with the bucket, ask the person to step further away.

Once the donkey is able to focus on the bucket, ask the person to step a little nearer. If the donkey disengages with the bucket to

scratch or move away, ask the person to wait until the donkey looks at the bucket once more. If he turns away for a moment, wait. He may well approach you once more to continue with the game.

Gradually ask the person to step nearer. Your donkey may be more comfortable if the person turns their body at a slight angle and looks down. Direct eye contact can be intimidating to a nervous animal.

Progress over several short sessions if necessary. When the person is close by, ask them to move their hand in the air. The moment the donkey looks away from the bucket, ask them to wait or lower their hand.

When the donkey is comfortable with the person standing next to the donkey with their hand slightly outstretched, ask them to stroke

Be mindful not to break the 'bucket contract'. Stop all interactions the moment the donkey looks away from the container.

or simply touch the donkey on his shoulder with the back of their hand.

Remember to pause or go back a step if the donkey looks away from the bucket at any point.

7. Introducing novel items in the field, stable or barn

Research shows that a high proportion of animal guardians and care-givers are likely to practise specific exercises for no more than ten minutes a day. It isn't always necessary to find additional time in a busy schedule to expand a donkey's education as many new experiences can be introduced by adapting the daily management and handling of the donkeys in your care. Giving donkeys the opportunity to explore novel items and to eat from different

containers can help build confidence in the safety of an environment they already know.

Considerations

Ensure that the donkey is not trapped by the novel item blocking his route to his shelter, place of safety, water or feed. Keep hold of any feed sacks or lightweight material that you take into the paddock in case they flap in the wind and spook the donkey.

The aim is to gradually expand the repertoire of toys, surfaces and food containers without flooding the donkey's nervous system with too much information in one go.

How to

Try using feed bowls of different shapes, size and colour. If your donkey hangs back from

Gradually build up the repertoire of new feed bowls, toys and games.

The nervous system learns from every experience, including sensory input through the soles.

the new item, sprinkle some treats or feed in his regular bowl as well as the new container and gradually move them closer together. Let him explore the new bowl at his own pace, and change the location of the new bowls on a regular basis whether you are using them in his stable or out in the pasture.

Set rubber matting out in the paddock or barn and apply the same technique using treats or fodder to encourage him to explore the new surface in his own time. Ensure he cannot pick up the surface with his teeth as this may frighten him if he rockets backwards and cannot let go.

Fill paper sacks or cardboard boxes with hay or barley straw and sprinkle a few treats inside. Ensure that any staples and tape have been removed. If the donkey cannot approach the box or bag, try using a smaller one instead, or cut it down so that it is less intimidating, until

your donkey is confident enough to explore the contents. You can also try placing the new item inside something that is already familiar to your donkey. Make sure he does not frighten himself by grabbing it with his teeth.

Fill large plastic milk containers with treats and let him watch you tip a few out into his stable or enclosure. Once he has learned to associate the containers with a reward, thread a lightweight rope through the handles and string several containers across a safe space, ensuring that he cannot get trapped in the rope. Let him approach the containers and watch him work out how to tilt the containers to release the treats. Avoid the temptation to help him out too much. The satisfaction of problem solving is often greater than the end result. Always remove the cartons and rope before you leave the enclosure.

Vary your clothing as you go about your usual

routine. Accustom your donkey to seeing you in different hats, coats, boots and so on. Carry novel items such as umbrellas or walking sticks past his paddock and move them quietly in the air. Avoid opening the umbrella too close to your donkey and ensure he has enough space to move away.

BODY-WORK FOR ALL

All the following exercises can be useful to extend a donkey's education, to enhance his well-being or as a thank you for the work he does. All donkeys are individuals, so tailor the body-work to your donkey's needs. Start wherever your donkey enjoys being stroked or gently scratched. This may be over his shoulders or the upper part of his back, or he may prefer you to begin with gentle hair slides on his mane if he isn't used to being touched.

Regardless of where and how you introduce the body-work exercises to your donkey, keep your hands relaxed and the movements calm and fluid. Tension in your own body can make your contact stiff and heavy. Remember that you are working with him, not doing something to him, and it is important that you progress at his pace.

If you are working with a donkey that is unhandled or difficult to catch, or is worried about contact on his body, you may need to start with the recommendations in the section on connecting with nervous and novice donkeys before progressing with the exercises listed here.

8. Introducing a single wand

Introducing the single wand is a simple and practical exercise to teach your donkey even if he is easy to catch and handle. As well as being a stand-alone exercise, it is the next step on from working with two wands as described in the section for working with novice and nervous donkeys.

As well as having many useful applications for day-to-day handling and for a variety of teaching and leading exercises, it gives the donkey's nervous system a new experience and can help engage the parasympathetic nervous system when used in a calm and mindful way.

Slow stroking with the wand can calm a fidgety or anxious animal and can help a donkey stand in balance for the farrier, or when having his hooves picked out or a leg injury treated. Using the wand enables you to initiate contact without crowding the donkey and to access no-go areas such as the hindquarters and lower legs without jeopardizing your own safety or increasing your donkey's concern by bending down or invading his space. It is also a brilliant way of working with a fearful donkey who hides behind a more confident friend, and has been a vital first step for teaching many members of the equine family that the presence of humans is nothing to fear.

Considerations

Avoid jumping to conclusions if your donkey is worried by the appearance of the wand. Donkeys that exhibit fear when a schooling whip is present have not necessarily been beaten in the past. Without doubt some animals are abused, but it is often the novelty of an object, suspicion, poor body awareness and sensitivity to contact that triggers the fear rather than the memory of a distressing experience.

How to

Put a headcollar on your donkey (if he is used to wearing one) and stand on his near side. Don't tie him up as it is important that he has the option to move if he is worried. A tied donkey accidentally startled by the wand may run backwards and injure himself. Take the rope or lead line in your left hand but avoid wrapping it around your hand. Hold the wand in your right hand. Keep a contact on the lead line to give support to the donkey, but avoid pulling on the line or forcing him to stand still.

Make sure you stand in balance and move through your whole body as opposed to simply moving your arm. If you are braced through your body, there is an increased likelihood of moving the wand too quickly and too firmly, which may unsettle or alarm your donkey. Remember to breathe. When we concentrate we tend to hold our breath and this can create tension in our own body, which can trigger concern and encourage bracing in the donkey.

Start by holding the wand as shown in the photograph. Contact on the chest can be very calming for the majority of animals. Unless your donkey is really worried by the presence of the

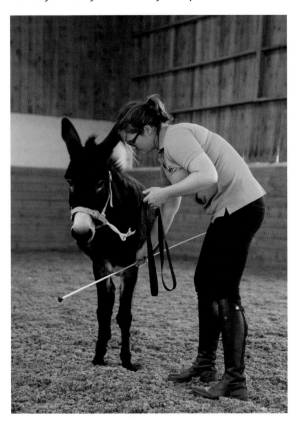

Stroke the donkey with the button end of the wand before turning it round.

wand, stroking him slowly on his chest from the base of the neck to the bottom of the chest with the button end of the schooling stick can be a safe and reassuring way to introduce the wand and most donkeys settle quite quickly when touched in this way.

Keeping the movement gentle and fluid, stroke your donkey on the chest two or three times. Pay attention to his body language as you touch him with the wand and note whether he widens his eye, goes into freeze, holds his breath, breathes more quickly, or starts to relax, softens his eye and lowers his neck. Quietly remove the wand after a few strokes and watch your donkey's reactions again. Does he move away, take a deep breath, turn to look at you and/or the wand, or step towards you? If he steps away, go with the movement and then invite him to step towards you again.

Repeat the exercise. As your donkey settles, extend the area that you are touching. Stroke the wand down the chest and the upper part of the forelegs and continue along the back. Monitor your donkey's reactions at all times, and remember to give him plenty of breaks. If he is really nervous, you may need to break down this exercise into several short sessions over a period of several days.

Switch sides so that you are standing on the donkey's off side and repeat the exercise. You will now be holding the lead line in your right hand and the wand in your left hand. Note whether this changes your donkey's responses, and how easy or difficult it is for you to work in this potentially less habitual way.

Once your donkey understands that contact with the wand is relaxing, you can turn the schooling stick around and use the full length instead of just the button end. Start at the chest again and stroke down the front of the forelegs, and then down the back of them. Be aware that your donkey may be more concerned as the wand will look and feel different when its full length is used. Remember that when we change one thing, we potentially change everything.

Gradually extend the parts of the donkey's body that you can stroke with the wand.

Build the exercise over time to develop confidence and trust. The aim is to be able to stroke the donkey all over his body, including along the midline and down the hind legs. If you touch an area that triggers concern, go back to an area where contact was acceptable and gradually work back towards the area that caused the anxiety.

9. Using different textures on your donkey's coat and skin

In general, a donkey that can be touched all over his body is more consistent in both behaviour and performance than a donkey that is sensitive to touch, but the introduction of a novel item can elicit a fear response in even the most confident donkey, particularly if he is under any duress at the time.

Some donkeys may prefer being touched by something other than the human hand if they have had poor experiences in the past, and using something as simple as a small round tack-cleaning sponge can be a useful first step in helping donkeys overcome any grooming concerns.

Accustoming your donkey to being touched with a variety of different textures will have far-reaching benefits and, as the nervous system processes different types of touch in different ways, we can give the more timid donkey many new experiences in the safety of his familiar environment. This is of particular benefit to donkeys that have had little education and are easily overloaded with the sights and sounds of the big wide world. Even if you do not intend to take your donkey out and about, and you handle him on a regular basis, there may be times when he needs to be tubed, treated for an injury, bathed or examined by a vet, using equipment that may be unfamiliar to the donkey, such as a mobile scanner or stethoscope.

Considerations

As with the ground-work exercises, body-work exercises are limited only by your imagination. You do not need to buy expensive equipment to give your donkey new and rewarding experiences. A variety of grooming brushes can be easily sourced, but mitts, car cleaning cloths, soft paint brushes, sponges, pocket hand warmers, and so on can also be utilized. It goes without saying that the items you choose should be new and should not have been in contact with any toxic substances or irritants.

You may be surprised at how something so seemingly insignificant and simple can advance the education of your four-legged friend.

How to

The nervous system continues to process sensory information long after the exposure to the stimulus has ceased. Work in small sessions using one or two pieces of equipment at a time. Use softer textures such as sponges and mitts on areas where the skeleton is closer to the skin, such as around the face, or when working with donkeys that are elderly, stiff or underweight.

Watch your donkey's responses to the different sensations. Depending on the item you have selected, gently stroke him on different parts of his body, or use the mitt or sponge to do the circular TTouches listed in this body-work section, or even a combination of the two.

If the donkey is worried by the introduction of a new texture, try holding it in one hand while you stroke him with the back of your other hand. Then stroke him again with the back of the hand holding the item, before you touch him again with the object that is causing him concern.

THE HEAD

10. Working around the face

Focused body-work on the face and around the head can be very rewarding for both you and your donkey. It can promote relaxation and calm, help release tension around

Introduce novel items one at a time and note whether the donkey turns his head or moves his body away. Pause and wait to see if the donkey re-engages, or give him a break and work over several sessions if required.

important anatomical structures, including the temporomandibular joint, the muzzle, across the forehead and round the base of the ears, and enable you to check for any sensitivity that may be linked to poor posture or dental imbalances.

Investing time connecting with your donkey in this way can also have practical applications such as helping donkeys overcome concerns about being handled around the face, reluctance to wear a fly mask or headcollar, or issues with being caught, bridled, led and tied. It is also a useful starting point for donkeys that do not like to be paste-wormed or have their teeth checked, and can help to develop trust as many fearful animals do not like to be touched around their head.

Considerations

If your donkey is nervous, you may need to start building his confidence by working on his neck or elsewhere on his body before progressing to more focused body-work around his face.

Donkeys often bump or push with their noses as a means of communication and to encourage a companion, whether four legged or two, to move out of the way. There is often a correlation between the part of the body that the donkey uses to express himself and sensitivity to contact around that area. Even if your donkey is generally confident he may dislike being touched around his muzzle, nose and face.

As you work quietly around your donkey's head, pay attention to his nervous system responses, and feel for any temperature changes and/or uneven muscle development. As you work around the poll (the bony structure between the ears), note whether it feels unlevel or crooked, and if the space between the bone and the base of each ear is equal or narrower on one side.

Always allow your donkey to move if he needs to and remember that biting, pushing, moving away, pinning his ears, stamping and so on are signs that your donkey is feeling worried. Watch for the smaller, more subtle signs that indicate your donkey is concerned and change what you are doing or give him a break before he has to become more expressive and 'shout'.

How to

Put a headcollar on your donkey and stand facing him and slightly to one side. Rest the fingers of one hand lightly on the noseband to support his head. Avoid gripping the noseband

as this restriction may make your donkey feel uncomfortable. A tight hold will also prevent you from releasing the contact quickly should your donkey suddenly move away, walk forward or push you with his nose. If your donkey is unsettled when you stand in front of him, hold the lead line in one hand and stand to one side. This will give your donkey more space and help him to feel more secure.

Keep your hand relaxed so that you maintain a natural soft flexion through the fingers and initiate contact with the back of the fingers. Start stroking your donkey quietly on the cheek, between the eyes, down the sides of his face and nasal bone, and up and over the forehead. Follow the direction of the hair using small, flowing movements and remember to pause. If you touch an area that gives your donkey cause for concern, move back to an area where contact was more acceptable and gradually work back towards the area that triggered the response. If he remains worried, change the direction or speed of the circle, the type of TTouch you use, or give him a break.

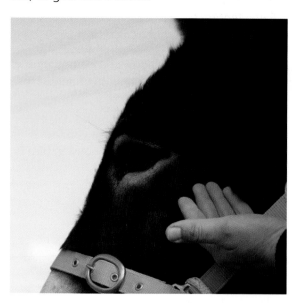

Use the back of your hand to initiate contact and check for warmer areas.

If you are standing to the side you will need to start stroking him on his cheek or on the side of his face. As he grows in confidence, you will be able to change your position and stand in front of him but do not be tempted to rush through this stage. Switch sides (or change hands) so that you can continue stroking the other side of his face. Note if his behaviour changes when you alter your position.

11. Chimp TTouch

If your donkey is enjoying being stroked around his head and face, continue with a different TTouch so that you start moving the skin in one and a quarter circles as opposed to sliding the back of the hand over the hair and underlying tissue.

Curl your fingers and make a soft, 'open' fist. Place the back of your fingers, between the first and second joints, on the side of his face or on his cheek. Gently move the skin in a smooth circular direction, as described in the Circular TTouch textbox. Avoid pushing with your fist.

Pay attention to the quality of the circular movement, and the mobility of the tissue beneath your fingers. You may find that the skin on one side of your donkey's forehead is more mobile than the other side, for example. Remember to pause between each TTouch and to move your hand slightly after each circular sequence.

12. Baby Chimp TTouch

If your donkey does not enjoy Chimp TTouch or if you are working with a little donkey, try changing the position of your hand and make

Curling the fingers and using the back of the knuckles or the back of your fingernails diffuses the contact for animals that are overwhelmed when touched with the palm or the back of the hand.

the connection with the back of your nails. This enables you to make contact with a smaller surface area, which may be more practical and/ or more acceptable to your donkey.

13. Working around the eye

Working around your donkey's eyes can prepare him in advance should veterinary examination and treatment ever be required for eye infections or injuries to the eye itself or to the tissue around the eye. It can also help keep the donkey calm should there be any debris that needs removing from or near the eye.

If you need to administer eye drops for any reason and haven't had the chance to set your donkey up for success in advance, you can use this technique before and after treatment. It will

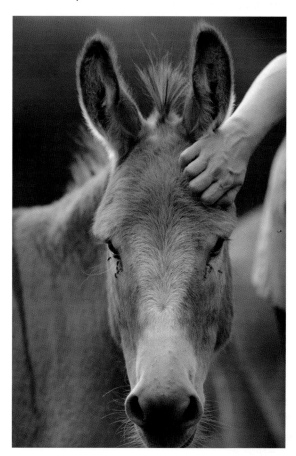

help to keep him calm and form a more positive association with eye medication.

Considerations

You do not need to spend considerable time working around the eyelids. Keep the contact light and gentle and incorporate this TTouch into the rest of the body-work on and around your donkey's head and face or as part of your grooming routine. Avoid doing this TTouch if you have long nails.

If your donkey is worried about being touched around a particular eye, consider how this might be connected to tension or sensitivity to contact elsewhere on his head, or to his concerns about being handled from a particular side.

How to

Once your donkey is settled with contact around his head and face, you can progress to working in a more focused way. Stand to the side or slightly in front, as described in the section on the head and face. Keep your fingers softly curled and alter the angle of your hand so that the tips of your middle three fingers make contact with the skin.

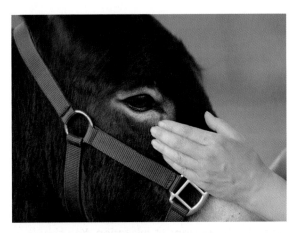

Accustoming your donkey to gentle TTouches around his eyes will help to keep him calm when contact in this sensitive area is necessary.

Using the circular movement, start working on an area below the bottom eyelid and gradually work your way up the face so that you do not take your donkey by surprise if he is not used to being touched around the eyes.

Work slowly and quietly around the eye, paying attention to his expressions and your own posture. Remember to breathe and keep the contact light. You only need enough pressure to gently slide the skin over the underlying facial bones.

If your donkey is happy, switch sides and work around the other eye or give him a break if he is showing signs of concern.

14. Working around the nostrils

Working around the nose, including inside each nostril, can be a useful starting place for donkeys that have concerns about being handled in and around the mouth. As with all the body-work exercises, it also has practical applications in preparing a donkey for any veterinary attention that may necessitate the use of nasal tubes for treating problems with the tear ducts, colic or choke.

Considerations

This may be a completely novel experience for your donkey. Donkeys have a really good sense of smell and use their muzzle and nose to communicate and to process information from the environment. Warm your hands if necessary before working around the sensitive muzzle.

How to

Stand to the side of your donkey and support his head by resting the fingers of your near hand gently on the back on the noseband under his chin or attach the rope/lead line to the side ring of the headcollar and hold the line near the clip. Avoid inadvertently pulling on the rope as this will affect his balance. Remember not to grip the noseband if your fingers are on the headcollar so that you can release the contact quickly should your donkey move.

Use the palm of your other hand to stroke down the side of his muzzle and around the nostril on the side nearest to you. If he is worried by contact from the flat of your hand, use the Chimp TTouch recommended for contact around the face.

Pay attention to any tightening of his chin or changes in the appearance of his eye and the set of his ears. Work slowly around his nostril. If he is settled, use your thumb and index finger to make small circular movements around the inside and outside edges of the nostril or stroke the outside edge of the nostril in a downward direction with your thumb.

Slide the tip of your index finger a little further into the nostril and continue with the circular movements. Switch sides and build over several sessions if necessary until your donkey is comfortable with, and enjoys, this gentle contact.

Donkeys use their noses to explore and as a means of expression. Teaching a donkey that contact around their nostrils is nothing to fear can increase calm and has practical applications.

15. Chin rest

Donkeys often rest their chins on the fence, on the top of their stable door, or on a friend when they are contented and relaxed. Working around the chin can promote calm and help to release tension around the temporomandibular joint and the upper part of the neck. It can also help you feel for, and address, any restriction in the movement of your donkey's head and neck.

Chin rests and TTouches around the chin can also help a nervous donkey to become more confident about being handled around the muzzle and to stay calm if an equine dental technician or vet checks for lateral movement in the lower jaw.

These exercises are also useful as a part of the education process when teaching young or unhandled donkeys to wear a headcollar or bridle.

Considerations

Avoid lifting your donkey's head when you introduce the chin rest and keep the movements within a comfortable range for your donkey. As with all body-work, ensure you are in balance and allow the movement to come through your whole body, rather than just your arm or hand.

How to

Stand on the left side of your donkey near his head, facing forward. If you are using a headcollar on your donkey, take the lead line in your left hand and gently cup your right hand around the chin groove. Meet the weight of your donkey's head in your hand, but avoid lifting his head. Support the weight of the head for a few seconds, or longer if your donkey starts to shows signs of relaxation. You should notice his eyes soften and his head becomes heavier in your hand.

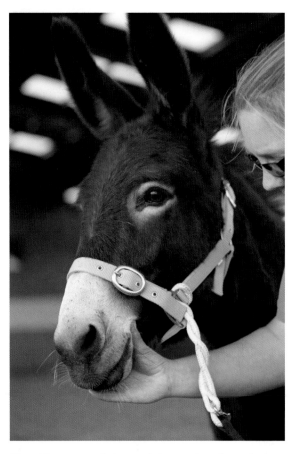

The chin rest can help to release tension through the upper part of the donkey's neck. Remember to soften your own arm to encourage the donkey to relax into your hand.

Slowly release the weight of your donkey's head from your hand. Allow him time to process by pausing for a few seconds before repeating the exercise two or three times. Note whether his head is lower when you finish the exercise than when you started.

16. Poll joint release

Habitual handling from one side and a natural lack of symmetry can reduce mobility through the donkey's neck. Fluid movement through the upper part of the neck is crucial for balance and well-being. This exercise adds a gentle lateral release to the chin rest exercise.

Considerations

Avoid pushing or pulling your donkey's head away from or towards you. Allow the movement to come through your own body and keep the range of movement minimal. The idea is to soften rather than actively flex the poll joint.

How to

Once your donkey has learned to relax with your hand under his chin, add a small fluid lateral movement. Stand in the same position and make sure you are balanced, with your feet slightly apart. As your donkey releases the weight of his head into your hand, slightly move the weight of your body onto the foot nearest your donkey. This will guide his head and neck away from you. The movement should be minimal and within a range that is comfortable for your donkey.

If your donkey is happy to maintain this position, pause for a moment before returning to your starting position with your weight equally distributed over both feet. Pause again and then transfer your weight onto your other foot, gently 'suggesting' that your donkey's head and neck should flex slightly towards you. Pause for a moment once again before returning to the starting position. Remember it is the quality and not the range of the movement that is important.

Note whether there is any disparity in the fluidity of the movement to left and right and consider how this might link with how your donkey organizes his body when led, ridden or driven. If your donkey fixes, braces or tilts his head in either direction, decrease the range of movement through your body, and therefore through your donkey's neck, when you try the exercise again.

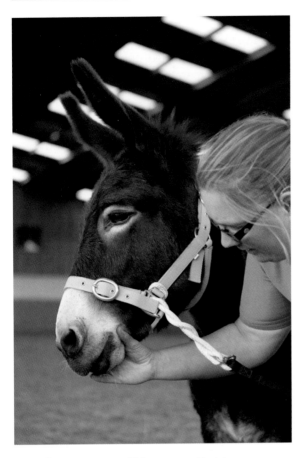

Keep the movement within a range that is comfortable for your donkey when softening the poll joint area. If the donkey tilts or raises his head, you have flexed his neck too far.

Cup your donkey's chin with the palm of your hand and gently move his chin in a one and quarter circle. Pause and repeat the movement after slightly changing the position of your hand so that you do not continually repeat the circular sequence on the same part of his chin. Move your hand quietly around the contours of his chin, noting if you can feel the muscles relaxing as you work. Try circling your hand both clockwise and anti-clockwise, and note whether the movement is more fluid one way than the other.

Donkeys that are tense, and those that become anxious, will often tighten the muscles in their chin. You can use the Abalone TTouch to help them relax and learn when in unfamiliar environments or when they are concerned.

The range of relaxed, free movement that your donkey is able to achieve should increase and become more equal to left and right as you practise this exercise over time.

17. Abalone TTouch

If your donkey cannot release his head into your hand with the chin rest, you can start by doing TTouches around his chin with the palm of your hand. As well as being a useful starting point for the chin rest, this exercise is beneficial as a relaxation exercise on its own.

Observe his head and the upper part of his neck as you do the TTouches on his chin and, as always, pay attention to his responses. If your donkey is relaxing, you should notice subtle movement around the poll joint and through his neck, and his eyes may soften and start to close.

If your donkey does not enjoy the sensation of your hand cupping his chin, try using the back of your palm or fingers instead. This will help to diffuse the contact and make the movements more subtle.

18. Mouth work

The mouth is connected to the limbic system, the area of the brain that is considered to be the control centre for the emotions and the gateway to learning (Daniel Goleman, 1996). This link is consistent with observations made by Linda Tellington Jones, who noted that many animals improve in behaviour, become increasingly calm and focused, and retain more information once tension around the mouth is reduced.

Tightening of the chin and elongation of the muzzle can be signs that the donkey is becoming concerned. Releasing tension around these areas can help to keep a donkey calm in a situation that may be causing anxiety or alarm.

Gentle TTouches both inside and around the mouth can help to stimulate the salivary glands, which in turn trigger the relaxation-promoting parasympathetic nervous system. This quietens the sympathetic nervous system responsible for the flight/fight response.

Mouth work also has the practical benefit of preparing a donkey for paste-worming, accepting a bit and having his teeth, gums and tongue checked for any signs of discomfort.

Considerations

A little mouth work goes a long, long way, and this is not an exercise that needs to be done on a regular basis unless you are working in small steps to help your donkey overcome any concerns about being handled around the mouth.

Donkeys that are emotional and insecure often have more tension around the mouth than donkeys that are more laid back and confident. If your donkey is anxious, start on another part of his body and build up to mouth work in small steps over several days or even weeks if necessary as contact on the extremities can be threatening for a fearful donkey.

If your donkey turns or lifts his head a little as you work, go with the movement. If he becomes really unsettled stop and go back to a body-work exercise that he enjoys before trying mouth work again.

How to

If your donkey is comfortable being handled around the head, and there is no danger of you being bitten or banged in the face, you can support his head by resting one hand on his nasal bone. If you are using a headcollar, rest your fingers on the noseband.

Stroke your donkey around the muzzle and chin with the flat of your hand. Move his upper and lower lips in small circles. If your donkey is calm, slide your index finger into the side of his mouth and lift the upper lip with the side of your finger. Keeping your fingers together and your hand angled slightly outwards will keep the upper lip raised and ensure you do not get bitten by mistake. Slide your hand back and forth so your index finger gently rubs the upper gum. If your donkey has a dry mouth, wet your hand first so that your fingers move easily. This will be more comfortable for you and your donkey.

Rubbing the upper gums can help donkeys remain focused and calm.

Pause for a moment to give your donkey time to process the sensation and watch his responses.

Stroke him around the chin once more and slide your thumb inside the lower lip ensuring you keep well away from his teeth. Work along the inside of his lower lip with your thumb. Next slide your finger inside his mouth, and up the inside of his cheek. Keep your finger well away from his teeth as he may bite you by mistake. Feel for any signs of possible damage from sharp edges on his teeth.

Draw the cheek slightly out to the side to minimize the risk of being bitten, and check the tissue for any signs that the donkey may be in need of dental attention.

19. Ear circles

Some donkeys are worried by contact on their ears. They may never have been handled around their extremities or may have dental issues or other health concerns that have caused some degree of sensitivity. If a donkey has been poorly handled in the past, he may have developed a negative association if his ears were pulled or twisted. Many donkeys that are worried about having their feet handled are also concerned about contact on their ears.

Ear circles are a useful starting point for ear slides and can give you more information about the mobility of your donkey's ears. They help to free tension around the forehead and poll joint area and can help donkeys overcome concerns about being caught and/or bridled.

Considerations

Donkey ears vary in size depending on the breed type so you may need to adapt this exercise to suit the conformation of your donkey's head and ears.

Even if dental issues have been addressed, your donkey may have restricted movement through the temporomandibular joint (the hinge point for the lower jaw) which can be a contributory factor to sensitive ears.

If your donkey dislikes having his ears touched, work little and often and start with other exercises on the body or around his face.

How to

Stand to one side of your donkey and support his head by placing the fingers of your outside hand lightly on the noseband of his headcollar or by holding the lead line. If your lead line is clipped to the side of his headcollar you will be able to maintain a better connection.

Work your way up the side of your donkey's face using the Chimp TTouch or run your hand lightly up the side of his neck. Cup the base of the ear nearest you between your thumb and index finger. Avoid gripping his ear. Keep your palm in contact with his body and slowly move your hand in a circular motion.

Pay attention to his body language and be aware of the mobility of his ear. Try circling your hand both clockwise and anti-clockwise. You may find that one direction is more acceptable

Circling the ear can help to release tension around the top of the head and neck, the hinge point of the jaw and across the forehead.

Switch sides and note once more if this elicits any difference in your donkey's responses.

20. Ear slides

Stroking the ear from the base to the tip can help lower heart rate and respiration, and, as well as being a rewarding way to connect with your friend, can calm and settle a donkey that might be in distress or upset. This exercise can also help to warm up a cold donkey that may not have been able to shelter from poor weather, or a donkey that is unwell.

Ear slides offer a brilliant way to prepare a donkey for any treatment he may require for problems such as ear infections, and can change his expectations of being touched around his ears he if has been poorly handled in the past. They offer a useful starting point for donkeys that are concerned when bridled or become worried when a fly mask is first introduced.

Considerations

Refrain from doing ear slides if a vet is checking your donkey's vital signs. If your donkey dislikes having his ears touched, start by stroking his ears with the back of your fingers or try covering your hand with a soft mitt.

to your donkey than the other. Pause for a moment and observe your donkey's responses. Repeat and switch sides, noting any difference in your donkey's response and/or the quality of movement.

You can progress to the next step if your donkey is comfortable and is enjoying this attention. Stand in front of him and slightly to one side. Support the noseband of the headcollar with the fingers of one hand, and place your other hand on his ear near the base. Circle the ear slowly and fluidly in both directions, within a range of movement that is comfortable for your donkey.

How to

Stand in front of your donkey and slightly to one side. Rest the fingers of one hand lightly on the noseband of his headcollar to support his head. Gently cup the base of the ear with your other hand and stroke the ear from the base to the tip.

Pay attention to the temperature of the ear and repeat the movement, altering your hand position slightly each time so you stroke the whole ear. Many timid donkeys have cold ear tips. Ensure you do not squeeze the ear.

Vary the ear slides by sliding your thumb inside the ear flap.

NECK, SHOULDERS AND CHEST
21. Mane slides

Stroking the mane can be very calming for donkeys and can help a fidgety donkey to settle and relax. It can also help to release tight skin through the neck.

This exercise offers a useful starting point for donkeys that are worried about having their ears handled or fear direct hand contact on their body, and as a preparation for trimming or brushing the mane.

Considerations

If your donkey is sensitive around his ears or his shoulders, start in the middle of his neck and quietly work your way up to the poll and then back down to the withers or vice versa.

Gently stroke the ear from the base to the tip, changing your hand position slightly each time to ensure you cover the entire ear.

How to

Take a small portion of your donkey's mane between your thumb and fingers, as close to

Remember to switch sides and note your donkey's responses as you work and also when you stop.

If your donkey is enjoying the ear slides, change your hand position so that your thumb is in contact with the inside of his ear as you work. This will enable you to check for any debris that may need removing.

If your donkey is tense through the neck, start the mane slides by stroking the tip of the hair before circling and stroking the mane from the base.

the crest as possible, and slowly stroke the mane in an upwards direction from the base to the tip of the hairs.

Note his responses. If he becomes unsettled when you stroke a certain part of his mane, go back to an area that he found more soothing and gradually work towards the area where he showed more concern.

Experiment by slowly circling the portion of mane you are holding before sliding your hand up the hair, and observe any movement through the skin on his neck.

22. Neck rock

Rocking the neck can release patterns of bracing and is a simple technique that can be used to help donkeys that fix through the neck or go into freeze when being handled, led or ridden.

Considerations

Although the exercise is called a neck rock, the movement is minimal and is more of a gentle wiggle of the tissue than a rocking motion. This isn't an exercise that needs repeating multiple times but is worth practising when the donkey

is relaxed so that the sensation of your hands on his neck doesn't increase anxiety when used for a donkey that displays any signs of concern.

How to

Stand to one side of your donkey, facing slightly forward. Place your near hand on the donkey's crest and your outside hand on the underside of his neck. Move your near hand towards you and your outside hand away from you, then guide the tissue back the other way so that your near hand moves the crest slightly away from you as your outside hand draws the bottom line towards you.

Remember to let the movement come from your feet and avoid gripping your donkey's neck. Vary the speed with which you gently

Gently wiggle the neck and observe your donkey's response as you move your hands towards the poll and back down to the withers.

wiggle the tissue and gradually move your hands up and down the neck, paying attention to your donkey's comfort levels at all times. Note his responses and feel for any resistance that may be present in the muscles. If your donkey cannot tolerate you cupping his neck with both hands, start by wiggling the top of his crest with one hand and build from there.

23. Clouded Leopard TTouch

This calming, circular TTouch is the foundation of all the circular TTouches. It can be used anywhere on the body but can be particularly beneficial when working around the vertebrae in the neck, around the jowl and in front of the shoulder, as well as all over the neck.

The Clouded Leopard TTouch can help to increase circulation through the skin and release bracing patterns that may inhibit the movement of the donkey to a greater or lesser degree. It also offers a pleasurable way of interacting with your donkey and can help a fidgety donkey to settle.

Tension in the skin can make injections, blood tests and/or microchipping more uncomfortable than they need to be. This lovely TTouch can be used before, during and after treatment and can help to change a donkey's expectation of what contact on his neck might mean.

Considerations

Pay attention to the quality of the circular movement as you work and remember to breathe. Keep the pressure light and move the skin around the imaginary clock-face, rather than sliding your fingers over the top of the coat.

If this TTouch appears to be uncomfortable for your donkey, try using the Llama TTouch or Chimp TTouch instead. Alternatively you could start with mane circles and slides before

progressing as these can help a donkey to become accustomed to the sensation of movement through the skin.

How to

It isn't necessary to put a headcollar on your donkey if you know he enjoys being touched but it can help to maintain a connection and support his head as you work.

Stand to one side of your donkey. Holding the lead line in your outside hand, place the finger pads of your middle three fingers on your donkey's neck. Where you start will depend on your donkey. Many donkeys are concerned by contact on the upper part of the neck so the middle of the neck may be more acceptable at first. Let your thumb and little finger rest lightly on your donkey's neck. Lifting any finger in the air can tighten the joints in your hand, which may make the contact from your finger pads less subtle.

Move the skin in a circular, clockwise direction, and pause before sliding your fingers to another part of his neck. If he is unsure about the movement, try varying the direction or speed of the circle. Note any changes in the mobility and temperature of the skin and the quality of his coat as you work.

Move the same piece of skin in one and a quarter circles then pause before sliding your fingers over the coat to repeat the circular TTouch on another part of the neck.

While it can be helpful to work from the top to the base of the neck in smooth, connected lines, the TTouches can be done anywhere. If your donkey has a poor association with hand contact on his neck, he may find it more acceptable if you do a few TTouches in different areas at first.

Remember to work on both sides of your donkey's neck if you can.

24. Coiled Python on the chest

Working on the chest can be very calming for many animals. Contact on the chest may be more acceptable for some donkeys than being touched elsewhere.

Considerations

Donkeys that have spent a great deal of time working on the forehand, have poor foot balance, engage in rough games or wear equipment (including rugs) that does not fit correctly can be highly sensitive around the chest. They may bite when touched here.

Mane circles and slides, wither rocks and/ or exercises for releasing tension in the neck may be a more appropriate starting point and will help to address any tension or discomfort through the pectoral, brachiocephalic or sternocephalic muscles that might be contributing to the donkey's concerns.

How to

The Coiled Python TTouch is a mixture of two TTouches: the Abalone and the Python Lift. Blending the TTouches together can give the nervous system additional new experiences and this TTouch can be particularly relaxing. Although we have listed it as a useful TTouch for releasing tension through the chest, it can be used anywhere on the donkey's body, as can the majority of the TTouches.

Stand to one side of your donkey, parallel to his shoulder. Although you can use either hand, you will probably be more comfortable if you use your left hand if you are on his near side, while holding the lead line in your right hand.

If you know your donkey is comfortable with contact on his chest, and you choose to do body-work while your donkey is at liberty, you can rest your right hand gently on his withers or the upper part of his back to maintain a connection.

Place the palm of your hand gently on your donkey's chest and move the skin in one and a quarter circles as described in the Abalone TTouch (*see* section 17). Pause for a moment as you complete the circular movement, then gently move the tissue slightly upwards, maintaining contact with the skin. Pause for a moment then glide the tissue back down.

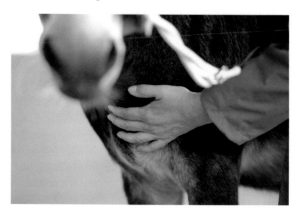

Contact on the chest can be very calming for many animals and can help to improve balance.

You shouldn't see much movement in your hand as the lift is minimal but you will probably notice a response from your donkey. Although this movement looks really subtle, the sensation can be quite profound.

Pause again before changing your hand position to repeat the movement on another part of your donkey's chest.

If your donkey is really sensitive, or you are

unsure as to how he might respond, support the lead line in your outside hand and start this exercise using the back of your other hand to diffuse the contact.

25. Sternum lift

As well as teaching your donkey to lift through the withers and lengthen his top line, this technique can help to strengthen weak muscles in your donkey's abdomen and hindquarters. You can also use this exercise as a foundation step for donkeys that struggle to back up.

Considerations

The aim is to encourage movement through the body while the donkey is standing quietly and not to ask him to step backwards on a cue. Keep the movement to an absolute minimum if your donkey is particularly stiff and/or weak, and remember you are inviting him to simply transfer his weight backwards and forwards while his feet remain relatively still. You may note, however, that he reorganizes the position of his legs as you influence his balance and improve his body awareness.

Keep your hand on the donkey's breastbone and transfer your bodyweight onto your front foot to encourage the donkey to lift through the withers.

If your donkey is sensitive to contact on his chest, use the Abalone TTouch (*see* section 17) along the underside of his neck and around his chest, and gradually build from there.

How to

Stand in front of your donkey, with one foot in front of the other, and place the palm of your hand on the centre of your donkey's chest. Imagine a thin, internal, flexible line passing from the centre of his breastbone, between his shoulder blades and on up to his withers. Picture your hand supporting the start of the line.

Move your bodyweight onto your front foot and visualize gently moving the line up and backwards at an angle so that it emerges through the top of his withers. Maintain the contact and pause for a moment. Slowly transfer your weight onto your back foot and allow the 'line' to return to its starting point.

Note the movement in your donkey's withers, back and abdomen. If he is generally supple, the movement should be fairly obvious. If he is stiff, or if your own technique needs a little refining, you may not notice much change in his posture at first.

Remember to breathe as you work and experiment by exhaling as you transfer your weight forwards, and breathing in as you rock slowly back.

Keep observing any engagement of your donkey's muscles as you work and ask for no more than two or three repetitions every other day. You will be amazed at how this subtle movement can improve muscle tone and flexibility in a relatively short space of time.

26. Shoulder delineation

Donkeys do not possess a collar bone. If a donkey is out of balance due to an injury, poor conformation, incorrect posture, irregular growth rates or our own habitual handling, the muscles around the shoulders can become tense. Movement through the shoulder can also be inhibited by ill-fitting equipment used on working, riding or driving donkeys and by rugs that are too tight.

This exercise is used in both TTouch and Connected Riding. It helps donkeys to release through the shoulder girdle and at the base of the neck. It can also help to improve gait and increase mobility through the fore- and hindquarters.

Considerations

If your donkey is braced through the shoulders, start with neck or wither rocks or try leading him over raised poles as described in the ground-work section. If he attempts to bite you, stamps a foot, pins his ears and so on when you try this exercise, he is letting you know that he is uncomfortable or concerned.

How to

Pop a headcollar on your donkey and take the lead line in your outside hand. Stand in balance with your feet apart and soften your knees to avoid bracing through your own body. Place the side of your other hand at the top of his shoulder, with your fingers pointing down the line of the muscles in front of the scapula. Avoid pressing into the tissue but use your bodyweight to lean slightly inwards while maintaining balance.

Glide your hand slowly down the front of the shoulder and note your donkey's responses at all times. If he finds this difficult, try inviting him to move his head slightly towards you without actively pulling him round. This can help to release any tension that may be triggering his concern.

Switch sides and pay attention to any differences that you notice between his left and

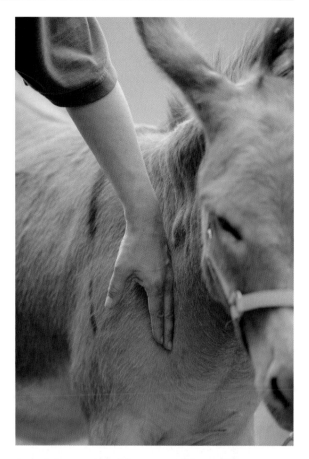

Lean into your hand (as opposed to pushing your hand into the donkey's neck) and follow the line of the shoulder to release patterns of bracing and tension.

right shoulders, including his responses as you work on each side.

27. Wither rock

Some donkeys find it really hard to transfer their weight from one foot to the other and many donkeys habitually load one foreleg more than the other. As well as helping to improve your donkey's overall balance, wither rocking can be a useful starting place for donkeys that find it hard to stand still, or struggle with the farrier and when his hooves are picked out. It can also help to encourage calm forward movement in a donkey that has gone into freeze, and will allow him to flex more evenly on both reins both in-hand and under saddle.

Considerations

Some donkeys may be uncomfortable when touched on the withers as a result of rough play, an accident, or ill-fitting equipment. If your donkey appears concerned when you place your hand on the top of his shoulders, try using a soft mitt to diffuse the sensation or move your hand back behind the shoulders.

How to

Stand to one side of your donkey, parallel to his shoulder, and facing forwards. Keep your feet

Transfer your weight from one foot to another to gently encourage the donkey to shift his weight from side to side.

slightly apart and rest the palm of your hand on his withers. Transfer your weight to the foot nearest your donkey, which in turn will transfer your donkey's weight to his foreleg furthest from you.

Pay attention to any resistance you might feel and pause for a moment with your hand resting on your donkey's withers before transferring your weight back onto your other foot. Repeat the movement two or three times and note whether your donkey's fetlock joints flex to the same degree on both front legs. If he has to step back or walk forwards as you rock his withers, does this only occur when he transfers his weight to one particular side?

If your donkey struggles with this exercise, try making the movement as small as possible. Remember that the aim is to gently alternate the way he distributes his bodyweight through his forelegs, rather than encouraging him to sway from side to side.

28. Shoulder press

This Connected Riding exercise can help to soften the donkey's neck, release tension through the shoulders and back, and engage his hindquarters. It is also a useful tool when leading a donkey that has either planted, or has set his neck and is bowling on.

It can also be used in situations where there is a danger that your donkey may kick out as it helps to bring his head towards you without using force and triggering more concern, and is equally beneficial regardless of whether you are working with your donkey in his stable, in-hand or under saddle.

Considerations

It is really important that you do not push your hand or fist into your donkey's shoulder and that you rotate your body to create the necessary movement. Remember to work within a range that is comfortable for your donkey and avoid too many repetitions.

How to

Put a headcollar on your donkey and clip the rope onto the side ring. Take the lead line in your outside hand. Face forwards with your feet apart, but with your body slightly angled towards your donkey, even if you are doing this as a static exercise. Soften your knees so your own movement is fluid and you remain in balance.

Make a soft fist with your right hand and place it in the middle of your donkey's shoulder. If your donkey is small, it may be more comfortable for you to use the back of your hand instead.

Place your fist or the back of your hand in the middle of the donkey's shoulder and pause before rotating your body away to soften the donkey's neck.

Rotate your hips away from your donkey. This movement naturally swivels your whole upper body, as opposed to simply twisting your shoulders. This neat rotation will take your near hand into the donkey's shoulder without applying unnecessary force, while the outside hand encourages a gentle flexion of your donkey's neck without pulling. Think of it as

inviting your donkey to soften and release, as opposed to making him bend.

Switch sides and look and feel for the quality of movement to left and right and note any disconnection through your donkey's body, such as tilting of the head, setting through the neck and so on. If he struggles, try decreasing the amount of rotation through your own body. Remember the aim is always to show the donkey's body what it can do, rather than reminding it of its limitations.

29. Caterpillar

This is another useful Connected Riding exercise that can be equally effective whether working with your donkey in the stable, in-hand or under saddle. It can help release tension through the donkey's neck and encourage him to soften and lengthen his top line.

Considerations

Remember to follow the line of the cervical vertebrae as opposed to working along the crest. Many donkeys will step forwards as you work up the neck. If he needs to move go with him, but if his pace picks up, take your hand away from his neck, ask him to stop and build up slowly by working on the lower part of his neck initially.

How to

Put a headcollar on your donkey. Working on his left side, support his head by resting your fingers lightly on the noseband or by holding the lead line up by the headcollar with your left hand. Regardless of your hand position, remember to think 'up' with your left hand to avoid pulling your donkey's head down by mistake when concentrating on the position of your other hand.

Place your right hand on the base of your

donkey's neck above the point of the shoulder. Flex your knees if necessary to lower your own posture to avoid bending low and bracing through your back. Your thumb should be on or near the jugular groove, and your fingers should be on the top ridge of the cervical vertebrae so that you cup the vertebrae with your hand. Start by sliding your hand up the line of the vertebrae to the donkey's ear, with the base or heel of your hand making the connection.

Trace the line of the cervical vertebrae with the edge of your hand to release tension through the donkey's neck.

Work slowly and experiment with the pressure. If you are too light, you may irritate your donkey but he may also find too much

pressure uncomfortable. If he is enjoying the sensation of your hand sliding up his neck, repeat this movement but this time lightly squeeze the tissue between your fingers and thumb as you work.

Remember to switch sides and note if his responses change when you work on the other side.

THE BACK AND HINDQUARTERS

30. Zebra TTouch

Every donkey is an individual and their backs vary from animal to animal depending on conformation, age and their past history. If your donkey has had several foals, has poor conformation and is croup high for example, has had an accident, or has been ridden in a badly fitting saddle and/or without consideration for the weight of rider that he could comfortably carry, you might notice that he or she is lordotic (sway-backed). Lordosis is also common in working donkeys that carry consistently heavy loads.

Arthritic changes in the appendicular or axial skeleton can also change a donkey's posture and although it may not be possible to reverse the damage that may have already occurred, it is possible to reduce the impact that it has on the rest of the body and improve the donkey's general well-being.

Tension in the back can lead to blocked awareness and anxiety during grooming, and the gentle sensation of your fingers working over the skin can help to increase circulation and change a donkey's expectation of what contact on the back might mean.

Even if your donkey is sound and has a good, strong and relatively straight top line, he may still have areas of tension through his back, particularly if he engages in rough play. Tension can make a donkey ticklish or reluctant to be groomed and a lack of core strength can also make it hard for a donkey to stand in balance on four legs, let alone three. This simple body-work exercise can therefore provide an important foundation step for donkeys that struggle with the farrier and when their feet are picked out.

As the back is a relatively large area compared to the legs and neck, the majority of donkeys will generally have a place on the back where contact is acceptable, even if they are concerned about being touched through the lumbar area for example. The zigzag movements along the back can help satisfy any itch without irritating the skin and are perfect for accessing sensitive or tense hindquarters.

Considerations

If your donkey is really worried by direct hand contact on his back, however non-invasive that contact may be, start by stroking him with the wand, using the body-work suggestions for the neck and shoulders, leading him through the labyrinth or simply walking in 'S' shapes to help free up his back.

How to

Stand to one side of your donkey, just behind the withers or parallel with his shoulder. Make sure you are standing in balance with your feet slightly apart and allow the movement to come through your whole body as opposed to just your arm and hand.

If you have a headcollar on your donkey, hold the lead line in your outside hand. Place your other hand behind his shoulder with your fingers pointing upwards towards his spine. Slide your hand up at a slight angle and open your fingers as you move towards the dorsal spinous processes, then close your fingers as you move your hand back down at an angle before repeating the movement along his back. Imagine you are 'drawing' multiple W shapes along his back with your fingertips as you work.

Draw your fingers together as you zigzag your hand towards the spine. If your donkey is small you can work on both sides of his body without changing your position.

Open your fingers as you move your hand down and over his ribs.

Avoid going over the top of the spine if your donkey lacks muscle through his back and watch his reactions at all times. If his back is well covered and your donkey is a small or standard breed, you can experiment by continuing the movement over his spine.

Avoid leaning on your donkey and move your feet so that you do not have to stretch and tip out of balance to reach the lumbar area, but remember to stay safe and out of range of his hind legs if you know that he kicks. If he shows concern at any point, go back to an area where the zigzags were more acceptable and gradually work towards the area that triggered the response. This may require several sessions.

If your donkey is fidgety or itchy, try working relatively quickly and slow the movement down as he begins to settle.

31. Troika TTouch

Some donkeys, particularly those that are anxious about being groomed or contained, dislike the sensation of their skin moving with the circular TTouches. Donkeys often appreciate a good scratch, but overzealous scratching in one area can trigger twitching in the muscles if tension is present.

The Troika TTouch is a circular, sweeping movement over the coat and skin. It is an excellent way to introduce contact in a form that may be more acceptable to a worried donkey, and forms a good foundation for grooming and general care. It is also an easier TTouch to master for people who may struggle to refine the lightness of the other circular TTouches that actually move the skin.

This TTouch combines well with the Zebra TTouch as a way to access no-go areas and to help engage and settle a fidgety donkey.

Considerations

Keep the movement light and fluid and your fingers soft and mobile. Locking your finger joints may make the contact more intense and uncomfortable for your donkey. Experiment with the pressure, but avoid digging your fingers into your donkey's coat and vary the speed as appropriate. A restless donkey may

settle more quickly if you make the movements a little faster initially. As he starts to settle, slow the movements down.

You can also use this TTouch around your donkey's chest, along his belly, and down his shoulders and the upper part of his hind legs.

How to

Stand to one side of your donkey, facing slightly forwards, and partially curl the fingers on the hand nearest him. If you are standing on his near side, you will be using your right hand. Use your finger tips or the first part of your finger pads to make the movements but allow your knuckles to flex as you work.

'Draw' two small circles approximately 5–6cm in diameter on top of each other on your donkey's coat with your fingertips, then move to another area by 'drawing' a bridge or a shallow rainbow from the top of the second circle before repeating the double circular movements. Work along your donkey's back and down his rump and repeat this movement all over his back and hindquarters. Remember to switch sides.

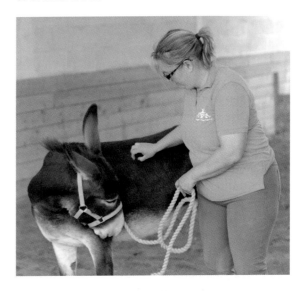

The Troika TTouch can be a useful introduction to grooming for donkeys that are body sensitive.

Pay attention to your donkey's body language and if he shows concern go back to an area where the Troika TTouch was acceptable. Gradually dip into the more sensitive areas over a couple of (or multiple) sessions as necessary. Experiment by mixing it in with other body-work TTouches if appropriate.

If your donkey enjoys this TTouch but is worried when you start to groom him, use the same pattern of movement with a soft rubber groomer, then with a body brush and build from there.

32. Back and croup rock

Donkeys that have a dropped back, are croup high, or suffer from arthritis or any physical problem that alters their overall balance can become blocked through the back. Even young donkeys may have areas of tension due to growth patterns or rough play.

Mobility through the vertebral column is crucial for well-being. Gently rocking your donkey through each part of the back will highlight areas where tension exists and enable you to encourage freedom of movement while improving balance, proprioception and good body awareness.

This exercise can be done in the stable or to encourage your donkey to move if he becomes stuck when being led or worked in-hand. As it teaches the donkey to transfer his weight from side to side, this simple technique can provide an important step for helping donkeys that struggle to remain in balance when asked to stand on three legs for the farrier or when their feet are picked out.

Considerations

Allow the movement to come through your whole body rather than just your arm and hand. The flexion left and right should be minimal but equal and fluid on both sides. Although you can

influence the donkey's back by standing on one side, it is worth experimenting by doing this exercise from both sides to see if this influences the degree of flexibility in any way.

If your donkey is really stiff, crooked or likely to kick, you may need to start with the wither rock combined with the Zebra TTouch. If he repeatedly cannot transfer his weight effortlessly on to one specific leg after a few sessions, consult your vet.

How to

Stand to one side of your donkey, just behind his shoulder and at a slight angle so you are facing forwards but can transfer your weight easily from one foot to the other. Hold the lead line in your outside hand or let your arm rest by your side if your donkey is at liberty. Make sure you are not within range of his hind legs if there is any chance of being kicked. Place the palm of your near hand on the dorsal spinous processes just behind his withers.

Move your weight onto the foot nearest your donkey and pause for a moment. Maintaining contact with your donkey's back, slowly transfer your weight on to your other foot. Remember to breathe. Think about rolling a tennis ball under your hand no more than a few millimetres left and right. The aim is to create a tiny ripple through the vertebral column as opposed to pushing and pulling the donkey from side to side.

Slide your hand a little further down his back and repeat this gentle rocking motion. Pay attention to the ease with which your donkey can alter his balance. You may need to move backwards as you work depending on the size of your donkey. If he walks forward, lifts his head, steps back, turns to nip, and so on, you have asked for too much movement.

If you feel resistance and your donkey feels 'stuck' at any point, go back to an area where the movement felt more fluid. If your donkey

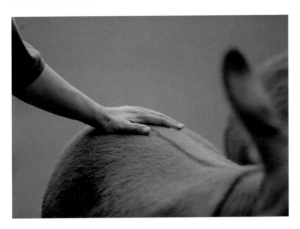

Cup your hand over the spine and transfer your weight from foot to foot to create a slight sway through your donkey's body as you work along his back to his hindquarters.

is free through his back you should notice a slight sway through his neck as you work. As you move along the lumbar area you may notice that there is naturally less movement in the lower part of his back. If your donkey is enjoying the back rocks, cup his croup with your hand and repeat this gentle movement on his hindquarters. This encourages slight flexion through his fetlocks and hocks and can help improve hind limb engagement and balance.

33. Jelly Fish Jiggles

This simple TTouch helps to release tight tissue and is particularly beneficial for donkeys that are stiff and lack mobility through the skin. It also provides a useful foundation for preparing a donkey to be clipped as the sensation is similar to the vibration of the clipper blades.

Considerations

Avoid pressing your hand into your donkey's body but ensure you maintain the contact

so that you actually wiggle the skin and do not simply rub your donkey's coat. Keep your fingers soft, your arm relaxed and your elbow slightly flexed to encourage suppleness in your hand.

How to

Hold the lead line in your outside hand or rest one hand on your donkey to maintain a connection if your donkey is loose. Place your other hand on your donkey's back and jiggle the tissue with your palm. You only need to create a little vibration on the skin. If your donkey is alarmed by this sensation, slowly glide the tissue from side to side at first and then try the little jiggle again.

Work all along his back and over his hindquarters in connected lines or on random areas depending on your donkey's preference. Note his nervous system responses at all times and pay attention to any temperature changes you may feel that might correspond with areas where the skin is tight.

If you are using this TTouch to help your donkey overcome concerns about being clipped, build up the exercise in stages. Place your clippers where your donkey can see them and use the Jelly Fish Jiggles on his back. Pay attention to his nervous system responses at all times. If he is calm, ask a friend to hold the clippers at a distance that is acceptable to your donkey and switch them on as you continue to work on his body with your hand.

Stop if the donkey panics at any point. Go back a step and build from there. Continue until you can hold the running clippers in your outside hand as you continue with the body-work. The next step is to switch them off and stroke him with the clippers. Continue with this exercise over several days if necessary until you can clip safe areas while your donkey remains relaxed.

34. Springbok

Although this TTouch used to be taught purely as a stimulating TTouch to help increase circulation and encourage engagement, it can have an incredibly relaxing effect on animals that find it impossible to settle and stand still.

It is a simple technique that can be used to help calm a fractious donkey in any situation, such as during veterinary checks and treatments or when his hooves are being trimmed, or as a way to establish and maintain a connection with a donkey that may be distracted by something that is causing him concern.

The Springbok TTouch can also help bring awareness to blocked areas where the muscles and skin are particularly tense and can be a useful starting point for donkeys that are worried about being touched as the actual contact made by your fingertips on the skin and coat is minimal.

Considerations

Keep the movement relatively light and allow your fingers to flex softly so that you do not inadvertently pinch your donkey's skin or pull his coat if his hair is long. Vary the pressure and speed until you find a rhythm that your donkey enjoys.

How to

Stand to one side of your donkey. Imagine that he has a light covering of dust sprinkled over his back and that you are going to lightly pluck the dust from his coat between your fingers and thumb. Your fingers and thumb will meet as you slide them off your donkey's coat.

You can use this TTouch in connected lines either side of your donkey's spine and along the rib cage or at different points on your donkey's body. If your donkey is a fidget or becomes worried when touched, you may find that random Springboks are more beneficial.

Make contact with the donkey's skin with your finger pads but avoid pinching or pulling his coat.

'Spring' your fingers off his skin and work in connected lines or in random places on the donkey's body.

You can use this TTouch anywhere on your donkey's body but it is most commonly used along the back and over the hindquarters as many animals carry tension in these areas. If you are holding your donkey for the farrier or vet and he is agitated, try using the Springbok on his neck to help shift his attention from the activity that may be causing the concern.

35. Working on and around the lumbosacral joint

The junction between the lumbar and sacral vertebrae is an important part of the donkey's anatomy. It enables efficient mobility through the hindquarters and allows the propulsion generated by the hind limbs to travel up the vertebral column. Sensitivity around the lumbosacral joint can trigger the donkey to drop his back when rugged or touched in this area, especially if he has skeletal or muscular changes due to injury, poor posture or disease.

While it may not be possible to address all the reasons for impaired mobility, it is possible to relieve some of the sensitivity that may result. In conjunction with other body-work and ground-work exercises that enable the donkey to move his body more efficiently, you can minimize the effects that such conditions may have on his overall posture by working around this area.

Run your fingers lightly along the top of the dorsal spinous processes until you feel a slight indentation under your fingers at the beginning of his pelvis.

Considerations

As with any physical problem, appropriate veterinary attention is paramount if you notice that your donkey is uncomfortable when you touch him around this area. For a donkey that is worried about being touched around his hindquarters, try using the Zebra TTouch along his back initially or cover your hand with a mitt to diffuse the contact.

If your donkey is sensitive around this joint, use a hand warmer to do the TTouches. Cover it with a cloth or let it cool a little if the temperature is too hot when the pad is first activated.

How to

Stand to one side of your donkey and hold the lead line in one hand. Stroke him gently along his loins with the palm of your other hand and watch his responses. If he is happy being touched around the lower part of his back, slowly run the first part of your finger pads along the dorsal spinous processes of the lumbar vertebrae towards his pelvis.

Keep the contact relatively light and avoid pressing down or rubbing your fingers along

the skeleton. You should feel a slight dip under your fingers where the lumbar vertebrae join the fused sacral vertebrae that form part of the pelvic girdle. Place your hand over the dip and pause for a moment. Remember to breathe. Move the skin gently in one and a quarter circles with your palm. If your donkey is comfortable and enjoying the contact, use the first and second part of your finger pads to move the skin in the same clockwise one and a quarter circles. Pause between each movement and work over and around the lumbosacral joint. Experiment with the direction of the circle if your donkey cannot settle and relax.

THE RIBCAGE AND BELLY

36. Lick of the Cow's Tongue

Growing juveniles, timid animals, donkeys with poor conformation, those that have been worked in ill-fitting equipment, older donkeys and breeding jennies can lose muscle tone through the abdomen and top line. Some donkeys may be sensitive to contact on their belly simply because they haven't been handled in this area or because they have restricted movement through the back.

This TTouch can help connect the donkey through his body and encourage engagement of core muscles. As well as being relaxing, this exercise is a practical step for donkeys that will be rugged up, ridden or driven.

Considerations

Keep the movement fluid and relatively light. Note your donkey's responses and pay attention to any areas of sensitivity as you work along his body. If he shows concern at any point, go back to an area where the sensation was more acceptable and slowly build from there.

How to

Stand to one side of your donkey and hold the lead line in the hand nearest your donkey's head. (You may find it easier to ask a friend to hold your donkey.) Place the palm of your other hand under your donkey's rib cage with your fingers pointing towards his mid line.

Although we usually start this exercise around the girth line, you may find your donkey is sensitive in this area. Start just behind the girth line if he finds that more comfortable and work

around the girth area when he has started to relax and trust the way you are interacting with him.

Maintaining contact with your donkey's body, bring your hand up and over his rib cage. Avoid lifting your shoulder as you work and turn your hand around as you glide your palm and fingers up and over his barrel. Your fingers will now be pointing towards his spine. Continue the movement until your hand is on the top of his back and slowly lift your hand from his

Maintaining the contact on your donkey's body, turn your hand around as you move up and over the rib cage and continue sliding your hand with your fingers pointing upwards to the top of his back.

Observe your donkey's reactions as you place the palm of your hand on or near the girth area.

Work along his body, provided he is enjoying the interaction.

body just before you reach his dorsal spinous processes.

Gradually work your way along his body repeating the same fluid, sliding movement. Note any subtle movement through your donkey's back.

37. Belly lifts with a wrap

Belly lifts can help donkeys release through the ribs, belly and back. They are beneficial for all donkeys, including breeding jennies, youngsters and the elderly. They help to encourage deep, rhythmical breathing, promote relaxation and are a useful starting point for donkeys that will go on to wear a saddle, pack or harness. The lifts can also help a working donkey overcome any concerns he may show when he is girthed.

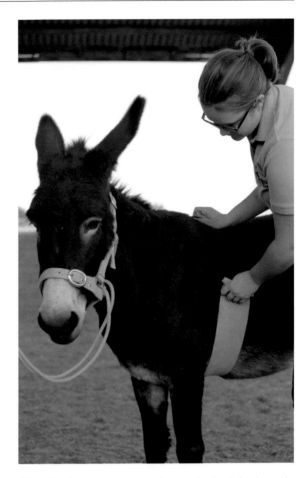

Place the body wrap around your donkey's body and pause for a moment to observe his response.

Considerations

If your donkey is sensitive to contact on the belly you will need to enlist the help of someone who can hold the lead line. Allow your donkey to look round if he wants to and remember to observe his responses at all times. If he is worried as you move the bandage to a specific area, go back and repeat the exercise where he showed less concern, before progressing with the lifts along the length of his body.

How to

You will need a long stretchy bandage, such as an exercise bandage or an Ace wrap. Start the lifts on the girth area if this is acceptable for your donkey. Hold one end of the bandage near the spine and bring the bandage gently under his body and around his rib cage with your other hand. With that hand, gently lift the bandage for a count of four. Pause, keeping the bandage in place for another count of four,

then gradually release the bandage for a count of six or eight. The release is the most important and influential part of the exercise.

Avoid pulling the bandage tight and remember to breathe. This exercise is more effective if you make a gentle connection with the donkey's ribs and belly rather than pulling all the stretch from the bandage. Experiment by exhaling as you initiate the lift, and inhaling as you release the wrap. If you breathe in as you lift, you may be more inclined to pull the bandage tighter than is necessary.

Move the bandage back an inch or so with both hands and repeat the exercise as you work

Lift the wrap slowly, pause for a moment then gradually lower the wrap.

way of helping a nervous donkey overcome concerns about having his legs and hooves touched and handled without the care-givers putting themselves in a potentially vulnerable position.

Even if your donkeys are generally confident, this exercise gives their nervous system a new experience and since even the most outgoing donkey can become momentarily concerned in a novel situation, this is a practical exercise to incorporate into your management routine from time to time.

Considerations

Allow the movement to come through your whole body as opposed to just your arm and hand, and start with exercise 8 'Introducing a single wand' before progressing to this step.

Practise stroking a table or chair leg with the wand to refine your skills before you work with your donkey to ensure that you do not press too hard or move the wand too quickly. Add a small rolling movement by rotating your wrist as you slide the wand down the leg to diffuse the sensation and to avoid the wrapped end bumping your donkey.

along the belly and the back. If you are working with a male donkey, remember to avoid covering his sheath.

THE LEGS AND FEET

38. Wand covered with a wrap

Wrapping a body wrap around the button end of a long dressage schooling stick and gently rolling the bandaged part of the wand down a donkey's leg enables you to initiate contact in hard to reach areas without having to crowd the donkey. It also offers a safe and practical

How to

Wrap an exercise bandage or Ace bandage around the button end of the schooling stick. If your dressage stick does not have a button end, the wrap may slide off.

Stroke your donkey's chest and down the front of his forelegs with the finer end of the wand. If you have already practised stroking your donkey over his body with the wand and he finds the contact enjoyable, you can turn the wand around after a couple of repetitions.

Hold the wand in the middle and stroke and partially roll the wrapped end gently down

Turn your hand as you move the wand down the donkey's limb so that the wrapped end of the wand rolls a little on his leg.

39. Rainbow TTouch

Anxious animals are generally worried when touched on the extremities and this natural and instinctive reaction is linked to the flight/fight response. Breaking down the handling of a donkey's legs into simple, logical steps can help even the most nervous donkey learn that contact on his limbs is nothing to fear.

This exercise breaks down the contact into small, easy-to-process stages and has helped many equids overcome their concerns.

Considerations

Sharing your life with a donkey that struggles when his feet are picked out or his hooves are trimmed may be frustrating at times but it is important to remember he is not being deliberately difficult. He may have poor balance, feel unsafe, or have discomfort or stiffness somewhere in his body that makes it hard for him to stand effortlessly on three legs.

Incorporate this body-work exercise into your daily handling routine and avoid the temptation to rush. Start on the upper part of the legs and vary the speed to see which is more acceptable for your four-legged friend. Some donkeys will accept faster movements more readily as there is less focused contact, while others may find slower TTouches more reassuring.

If you know your donkey is worried by contact on his hooves, invest more time working above the knee before trying to touch him on the lower legs and feet.

How to

Stand to one side of your donkey and rest the back of your hand on his shoulder. Maintain a consistent but gentle contact and avoid pushing your hand into your donkey's muscles and/or skin.

Gently glide your hand in a rainbow arc backwards and forwards over his coat and skin,

your donkey's chest and the upper part of his front legs, one at a time. If he shows any signs of concern, go back to stroking with the unwrapped end and then try again. Remember to drip feed the information into his nervous system a little at a time.

Continue down the front of each leg, noting whether you can increase the area that you are touching. Remember to go back one or two steps or give the donkey a break if he shows any signs of concern. It is often in the break that most change occurs.

Build on this exercise until you can stroke/roll the wrapped end of the wand down all four legs and ultimately over each hoof.

slowly lowering your hand down the side of his leg as you work. If he lifts a leg, raises his head or steps away, stop the movement and pause for a moment before going back to an area that was more acceptable to the donkey.

Use the Llama TTouch to change your donkey's expectation of what hand contact on his legs might mean.

Work in micro-sessions and try interspersing the rainbow patterns with quiet strokes on the front and back of his fore limb with the back of your hand. Make sure you are safe at all times.

If your donkey starts to panic as you bend down to reach his lower leg, break the exercise down even further and teach your donkey that bending down does not necessarily mean you are going to touch his leg. You can bend over and give him a treat, reach down to pick him

some tasty grass when you are walking him in-hand, or simply intermittently lower your posture as you move around him in the field or in his stable.

Once your donkey is able to relax as you do the Rainbow TTouch with the back of your hand, try repeating the exercise using the palm of your hand. Remember to build slowly over several short sessions if necessary. Your donkey may have developed a strong negative association with the sensation of the palm of the human hand on his leg if he has been forcibly handled in the past.

When you are working on the back legs, ask a friend to hold your donkey and stand facing backwards. If there is any danger that your

Once your donkey is settled, use both hands to make alternate rainbow patterns down his legs.

donkey will kick, you can make the rainbow movements with a covered wand once you have taught him the appropriate 'wand covered with a wrap' exercise.

When he is comfortable with the sensation of the Rainbow TTouch with one hand, place both hands gently around his leg and use them to make small alternate rainbow movements together. Take one hand forwards as the other hand moves back on either side of his leg, and repeat the arc pattern, moving your hands backwards and forwards gently down his limb.

40. Python Lifts

This Tellington TTouch body-work exercise can help to increase circulation to the lower legs and encourage more even weight distribution through the limbs. It is another practical exercise to help fearful donkeys overcome concerns about being handled on their legs and can help to improve balance and proprioception in any donkey, regardless of age.

Try this exercise if your donkey has been lame and now moves with a shortened or uneven gait even though the vet has given him a clean bill of health, or if you notice that your donkey habitually knocks a pole with the same toe or toes when working in-hand.

Python Lifts are also beneficial for donkeys that have spent time travelling or have been kept in the confines of a stable due to poor weather or ill-health, as well as for those that trip or have reduced mobility through their leg joints due to physical problems or old age.

Considerations

Build slowly and work through the other exercises for handling a donkey's leg if you know your donkey has concerns. Although both hands gently cup the leg at the same

time, some donkeys may prefer it if you only do the lifts with one hand. If your donkey is really worried by the warmth of your palm, try using the back of one hand instead.

How to

Place both hands on either side of the upper leg. Using just enough pressure to support the tissue, gently move the skin slowly upwards. Avoid gripping the leg too tightly, forcing the skin upwards or lifting the skin as high as it will go. Keep your thumbs parallel with your index fingers to avoid them inadvertently pressing into the donkey's leg.

Pause for a few seconds and slowly glide the

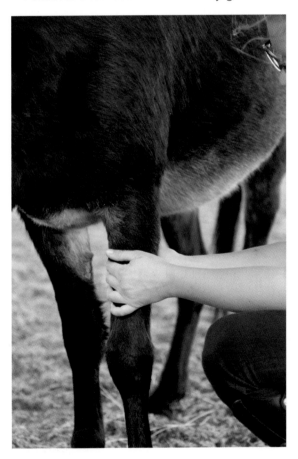

Cup the leg gently and ensure your thumbs do not press into your donkey's skin as you move the tissue up and down.

skin back to the place where you started the lift. Pause again, then slide your hands slightly further down his leg and repeat. Continue down the leg, keeping the movement flowing and rhythmical (provided this is comfortable for your donkey). If he lifts his leg or shows any other signs of concern, go back to an area where the lifts were acceptable and practise this exercise over several days if necessary until you can work down to, and around, the fetlock joint.

You can vary this exercise by using a combination of other TTouches on his legs.

41. Leg circles

Circling a donkey's legs has many practical applications. Some donkeys can stand on three legs but panic when the raised limb is moved or held in the air. Tension in the shoulders, neck, back or hindquarters can make it hard for a donkey to stand in balance and restriction through the neck or through the lumbar area can inhibit flexion through the fetlock joints in the fore and hind limbs.

Circling a donkey's leg can increase flexibility through the shoulders, neck and back and can improve gait and length of stride as well as proprioception. They can be done when the hooves are picked out or as a tool to help a donkey that may find it hard to stand in balance for the farrier.

Considerations

It is imperative that the donkey's legs are not taken out to the side when the leg is circled or even simply being raised. Donkeys are base-narrow animals and the majority of donkeys are relatively small; inadvertently abducting the limbs when the leg is lifted can be a trigger for anxiety and concern. The likelihood of drawing the leg out to the side is increased if the donkey is short in stature and the handler is tall. Flexing

your knees as you work will protect your back and make it easier for you to lower your body more effectively while remaining in balance.

How to

Stand to one side of your donkey and ask him to lift the foreleg nearest you. He may find it easier to lift his near (left) fore but if he has had poor experiences in the past, he may find it less threatening if you start on his off (right) side as it may change his expectation and help him to think through the steps rather than simply react out of fear.

If you are working on his near side, bend your knees and cup his fetlock with your left hand. Support his hoof with your right hand

Keep the toe pointing to the ground and slowly circle your own body to create movement in the leg.

and ensure that you do not draw his leg out to the side or ask him to lift it too high as this will increase the flexion through his knee.

Circle your own body so that you gently rotate your donkey's leg as you move. Imagine the spot where his hoof would be if it were still in contact with the ground, and gently circle his hoof over this area. If he fidgets, gently rock his hoof a little, but if he really panics let him place his foot back down.

Slowly circle the leg in both clockwise and anticlockwise directions and pay attention to the ease with which it moves.

Repeat the exercise with each leg and note any heaviness or stiffness that may be present in one or more of his limbs. When circling the hind

Support the hind cannon and hoof and repeat the same circular movement with the hind legs.

legs, it is not necessary to support the fetlock joint owing to the different joint structure of the hock. Support the hind cannon bone with your near hand instead of the fetlock as you hold the hoof with your other hand.

THE TAIL

42. Hair slides

Donkeys use their tails to express themselves but the position and appearance of the tail can also give you some clues as to his physical well-being. Tension through the back can trigger sensitivity in the tail and many nervous animals are worried about being handled around the tail and hindquarters. Releasing tension in the tail can help donkeys move beyond the instinctive flight/fight response and improve flexibility and balance.

Some donkeys that dislike contact on the head may accept touch on their tails and this exercise offers a useful starting point for donkeys that are worried about being handled around their muzzle and face.

Considerations

Many donkeys that kick are worried by contact on the tail. If you know your donkey is likely to react to a novel or worrying situation by kicking out with his hind legs, start by working your way through the body exercises for the neck and back, including the exercises for introducing wands.

How to

Use the Zebra TTouch along your donkey's back so that you do not take him by surprise. If you are standing on your donkey's left side, place the palm of your left hand on the wing of the pelvis; this will enable you to feel for any tension or movement that might indicate your donkey is concerned. Use the fingers of your right hand to do the hair slides.

Gently take a small amount of tail hair between your thumb and fingers and stroke the hair from the base of the hair to the tip even if the hair at the top of his tail is really short.

Stroke small sections of the tail hair and gradually work your way down his tail.

Avoid leaning over your donkey to work on the other side of his tail. Switch sides and remember to observe his responses at all times. You may notice his respiration increases or that he goes into freeze. If he displays any signs of concern, go back to any exercise he found more comfortable and build from there.

43. TTouches down the tail

Some donkeys may have been pulled by the tail or made to move or stand by someone twisting or lifting their tail at some point in their lives. Damage to the tail can result in remodelling of the caudal vertebrae and sensitivity to contact owing to strain within the

bone itself as well as in the periosteum that envelops the bone.

Handling a donkey's tail with care can assist with grooming, temperature taking, internal examinations, and as a preparation for sheath or udder cleaning, and careful handling can change a donkey's expectation of what contact on the tail may mean.

If a donkey is worried by contact on his tail he may also be sensitive to contact on his hind legs. Releasing tension through the tail can therefore be a useful step as part of building confidence when teaching a donkey to lift his hind limbs.

Considerations

Begin with hair slides. As with all the exercises, remember to work slowly and observe your donkey's responses at all times. Ask a friend to hold your donkey if you cannot work while your donkey is at liberty, but always allow your donkey the freedom to move away if he is concerned.

How to

Once you have introduced hair slides, you can use your fingers to make small circular TTouches down the tail.

Stand to one side and cup one hand around the top of the tail. Keep your other hand on the wing of the pelvis for support and to feel for any tension that might indicate your donkey is concerned. If your donkey clamps his tail, cup the top of the tail and wait for a moment to see if he relaxes or use the Abalone TTouch (*see* section 17) to help him relax.

Alternate with using your finger pads to do Clouded Leopard TTouches down one side of the tail, with the pad on your thumb working on the other side of the tail. Work your way gradually down the length of the tail bone, remembering to pause between each TTouch.

Take the tail in your hand and use your thumb or fingers to move the skin in small one and a quarter circles on both sides of the tail bone.

You can also try Python Lifts, with your thumb and fingers gently moving the tissue up and down the tail. Start at the base of the tail and work your way down to the end of the tail bone.

44. Stroking the tail

Stroking the tail can help to reduce tension in the back and encourage the donkey to soften and release through the neck. It can also help improve balance as many donkeys that are stiff will carry their tail to one side or have reduced mobility through the tail.

Considerations

Work slowly to build confidence and note if his responses change as you touch the different parts of his tail. Stroke the tail in a downwards direction and avoid lifting the tail too high as you work so that you do not raise it out of its normal range of movement. The set of a donkey's tail is different from that of a horse or pony and the tail does not flex in the same way.

How to

Rest your hand at the top of your donkey's tail, as described in the previous section. If he settles with your hand on his tail, curl your hand gently around the tail and stroke the entire tail from the top of the dock down to the end of the tail bone.

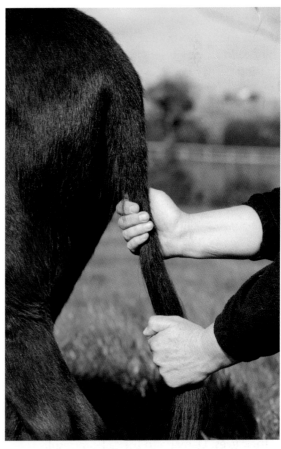

Make sure you do not lift the tail as you move your hands down the caudal vertebrae.

If your donkey remains relaxed with your hand around his tail bone and he does not kick, stand behind him and take the tail in both hands. Pass one hand over the other as you stroke the entire tail with your hands and gradually work your way down the length of the tail bone.

Remember to pay attention to his responses at all times.

BODY WRAPS

Body wraps are an integral part of the Tellington TTouch technique. Depending on the type of wrap that is used, they can improve proprioception and therefore gait, can help an anxious donkey to settle, encourage hind limb engagement, promote relaxation and improve mind/body awareness. They are also a useful starting point for introducing rugs, driving equipment and girths.

There are many ways to use wraps, and we recommend that you purchase Ace wraps, which are available online. Alternatively, you can try using elasticated exercise bandages but make sure that they are long enough, as the aim of the wrap is to increase awareness and not restrict movement in any way.

45. The Half Wrap

You will need two or three 10cm wraps for a Mammoth donkey or two 7.5cm wraps for a standard or small donkey. Start by tying one wrap around the base of the donkey's neck. This is called a Base Wrap and is the cornerstone of all the body wraps. Most equines accept this relatively quickly but if the donkey is sensitive to contact around the chest due to poor posture or an ill-fitting rug or breast collar, he may have a negative association with anything that goes around this part of the body.

Lead your donkey around the yard or arena while he is wearing the Base Wrap so that he becomes accustomed to the sensation before you attach the second wrap. You may notice

The half wrap.

that he slows his pace if he has a tendency to rush or starts to lower his neck and head. If he is happy with the Base Wrap, you can tie the second wrap to the Base Wrap on the right side of the donkey by the top of the shoulder or attach it to the Base Wrap on the donkey's left side and gently slide the Base Wrap around his neck so that the second wrap is now on the donkey's right side.

Bring the remainder of the wrap underneath the donkey's rib cage so that it is around the girth area. Attach it to the Base Wrap near the top of the shoulder with a quick release knot. Be careful if your donkey is girthy, is worried when rugged up or has never worn anything on his body before. You may want to experiment with belly lifts if you have any concerns that your donkey may not tolerate the Half Wrap.

The Half Wrap is a useful stepping stone to introducing a surcingle or a girth and can help to slow a donkey that rushes or works habitually on the forehand. It can also be useful for donkeys that find it hard to stand still and can be used for all the ground-work exercises.

46. Full figure eight wrap

The Full Wrap is beneficial for donkeys that are worried about walking through narrow spaces, slow loaders and those that lack hind limb engagement, stumble or spook. It is also a useful foundation step for donkeys that are not accustomed to wearing rugs or tack.

Considerations

Ensure that the wrap around the hindquarters does not ride up under the tail and worry the donkey, and avoid pulling the wrap too tight. It only needs to give information to the sensory system and should not restrict the natural movement of the donkey.

How to

Ask someone to hold your donkey and tie two wraps together to make one long length. Stand on the left side of your donkey and pass one end around the base of his neck and hold it at the withers. You should have the short end in your right hand. Switch hands so that the short

The full figure-eight wrap.

end is in your left hand and uncurl the rest of the wrap.

Cross the wrap over in an X just behind the wither and tie the ends together with a quick-release knot. You should now have a figure of eight shape. Slide the large loop around the donkey's hindquarters, ensuring that the knots lie on soft tissue and not on top of the spine. Gently move his tail from under the wrap.

Ask your donkey to step forwards and give him time to process the sensation of the wrap. Ask him to slow and halt, and note any changes in his gait or responses. If he goes into freeze, continues to rush after a few seconds or you notice a significant change in his gait, remove the wrap and gradually introduce it over several sessions if necessary.

GROUND-WORK EXERCISES

47. The headcollar and lead line

A well-fitting headcollar is important for the comfort of your donkey when working him in-hand. Many standard equine headcollars are too big around the noseband and have a tendency to slide to one side, which can pull the cheekpiece into or over the donkey's eye. The webbing may also be too wide if your donkey has a naturally narrow frame.

You can be more subtle and work on refining the signals you teach your donkey if the headcollar can be adjusted to be a comfortable fit. As you will be working from both sides of your donkey, ensure that the headcollar you choose to use has a ring on both sides of the nose piece.

Remember that your donkey's education does not begin once he is kitted out and ready to be worked in-hand. It starts from the moment you open his stable door. If your donkey is generally at liberty and able to move between the pasture and stable without being led, he may associate the headcollar

with something he deems to be unpleasant, especially if you only use it when he is in need of the farrier or the vet. Remember to use the headcollar for pleasurable interactions, even if it isn't really necessary.

Be mindful how you put his headcollar on and avoid flipping the headpiece over the top of poll joint area in case the end of the strap flicks him in the eye or on the neck.

The Zephyr lead – a soft lead line made specifically for use with TTouch techniques – is perfect for donkeys. The clip is small and light,

Hold the head strap and the buckle on the cheekpiece and lift the headcollar over your donkey's nose (as opposed to flipping the headpiece over the donkey's neck).

and the length of the line allows the handler to work closely with the donkey, or give him more space as and when required.

It isn't necessary to use to a TTouch lead line in order to work effectively with your donkey in-hand but be aware that many lead ropes designed for horses are actually quite heavy. It is therefore worth purchasing a pony lead rope if you can find one as the clips are smaller and the rope is slightly thinner, which makes it lighter and less cumbersome overall. Always remember that any equipment added to a donkey's body will affect his balance to some degree.

If you do not own a TTouch line, try using a length of climbing or magician's rope instead of a more traditional lead if you want a lighter, longer line.

Although lead lines are usually attached to the central ring at the back of the noseband, clipping the lead line to the side of the headcollar can be more beneficial when working with your donkey in-hand. It can help you to give more refined signals on the line and support the donkey's head more effectively if he is out of balance, while minimizing the chances of any pressure being inadvertently applied to the sensitive poll joint area. Downward pressure

Wrap the rope around itself and clip the line on to the triangle where the rope is attached to the webbing.

Thread the lead line through the buckle as shown to prevent it from tipping into the donkey's face.

on the headpiece can trigger bracing and elevation of the donkey's head owing to natural engagement of the opposition reflex.

If you are using a TTouch Zephyr lead, thread the line through the side ring of the headcollar as shown in the photographs. You can wind the rope around itself and attach it to the triangle or thread the rope section over the noseband if your donkey has a tendency to poke his nose and march forward. It is imperative that the rope is threaded over the noseband to prevent it from tightening around the sensitive nasal bone.

If your donkey is forward-going, loop the line over the noseband and attach it to the ring by the jowl; this configuration can help the donkey to soften through the poll joint.

If you are using a length of rope, attach the line to the side ring with a quick-release knot but ensure that the edge of the hardware on the headcollar does not tip into the donkey's face when you give a signal on the line.

If you are leading your donkey from his near side, hold the line in your right hand, palm up, and take the end of the line in your left hand. If your line is long, create a loop in the line and hold the excess line between your first and second fingers. Regardless of the type of leading equipment used, it is important that you do not wrap any part of it around your hand. If your donkey suddenly shoots forwards or backwards, the loop will tighten and you could be hurt. Ensure that no part of the line is dangling close to the ground, creating a potential trip hazard for you or your donkey.

The position of your right hand in relation to the clip of the lead line will depend on your

Take the end of the line in your outside hand with a loop between (but not over) your first and second fingers and hold the line with your nearest hand, palm up.

donkey and the exercise you are teaching at the time. Most donkeys prefer to have more space between them and their handler than we might initially think.

48. Stroking the lead line

This simple technique is an adaptation of Peggy Cumming's Connected Riding work and is a highly effective way of helping donkeys to release through the neck when being led.

Stroking the lead line can help a donkey turn more fluidly and efficiently in-hand, encourage a hesitant donkey to step forwards, or steady a donkey that may lean into the headcollar and walk briskly when concerned.

Timed correctly, it can be a useful technique to use when leading a donkey across or near grass and avoids the necessity to exert excessive force if the donkey tries to snatch a mouthful.

This exercise also helps to reduce bracing in the handler's arms and shoulders.

Considerations

If your lead line is coarse to the touch, avoid this exercise or wear gloves. Maintain a gentle connection on the line as you stroke but avoid pulling your donkey's head to the side.

How to

Stand in balance and make a gentle connection with your donkey through the lead line without

Flex your body and avoid staring at the donkey as you stroke the lead line.

Stroking the line encourages the donkey to soften and flex through his whole body rather than trying to turn him by simply moving his head.

pulling or creating excessive tension on the line. If your line is too slack this exercise will be ineffective.

Quietly stroke the line by moving your right hand slightly down the lead and passing your left hand underneath to pick up the line where your right hand started. Stroke the lead with the left hand as you release the line from your right hand. Pass your right hand under the line and repeat keeping the movements slow and rhythmical. Stroke the same part of the lead each time and avoid creeping up the line.

Be aware of your own body posture and position as you stroke the line. If you are using this neat little exercise to encourage a donkey to step forwards or turn, be mindful to look in the direction that you want to go. If you face the donkey and try to draw him towards you, you may confuse him or inhibit his ability to move by blocking him with your own body.

49. Walking the 'S'

Walking the 'S', or serpentine, helps the donkey to soften and release through the body and encourages the ribs to open and the back to lift. It can help to establish a more even rein contact for donkeys that are ridden or driven, and improves balance and proprioception by encouraging more even weight distribution through the limbs.

This Connected Riding exercise can be done in-hand or while walking your donkey out to and in from the field.

Considerations

The turns, both left and right, come from the position and movement of your whole body, not just your arm. Before you try this exercise with your donkey, practise rotating your body left and right. It is important to swivel through your entire pelvis as well as your trunk and not just twist your shoulders. It is these rotations

Even if you can only lead your donkey from one side, walking an 's' to and from the field will help to improve balance and flexibility.

The movement comes from your own body as you rotate right and left.

that help to encourage your donkey to release and flex.

Avoid pulling your donkey round, or pushing him away through the turns. The aim is to keep a light connection through your hand and to encourage the donkey to soften and yield in a fluid movement.

How to

Stand on your donkey's near side and support his head with your right hand. You can either hold the lead line next to the headcollar or hook your fingers through the noseband. Be aware of your own balance and ensure that your knees, hips and back are soft.

The S starts with you rotating to the right and inviting the donkey to turn away from you as you walk. Start by making the loops of the serpentine shallow. Asking for too much flexion initially may encourage your donkey to brace or tilt his neck when turning, without releasing.

Walk four or five strides to the right, then, as you continue to walk, slowly rotate your body away from the donkey and take four or five strides to the left. Repeat this pattern. If the donkey is able to release with ease, gradually increase the depth of the loop. As the depth of the loop increases, you may need to step back a stride when you rotate to the left.

50. Teaching a halt/stand

Although donkeys are generally quite adept at standing still when snoozing in the sun, resting in their stable or processing information, not all donkeys can stand on cue. Having the freedom to choose a specific behaviour is not the same as demonstrating that same behaviour when asked.

Like all animals, donkeys learn through associations, motive and reward, and your donkey may have inadvertently been taught that the headcollar or bridle means 'yahoo, we're on the move'. He may be keen to come in from the pasture or in a hurry to explore the excitement of the great outdoors. An inability to stand on cue may also be linked to discomfort, poor balance or anxiety.

Teaching a donkey to stand has many obvious practical benefits. If he cannot stand when there are few distractions, it is less likely that he will be able to remain calm and quiet in a busy environment or when the farrier or vet pays a visit. It is also far easier to open gates and stable doors or put on or remove equipment from a donkey that has learnt a little patience, self-confidence and self-control.

Considerations

If your donkey struggles to stand, try to think about all the reasons why this may be a challenging request. Set him up for success by asking him to stand on level ground for no more than a split second if this is all he can manage at first, and then invite him to walk on with an appropriate quiet cue before he starts to fuss and fidget.

Once your donkey can keep all four hooves on the ground at the same time in a quiet environment, generalize the exercise by asking him to stand in a variety of situations and locations around your property. Incorporate some of the ground-work exercises such as the labyrinth, walking the 'S' and zigzag to help improve his confidence and balance, and try using the Springbok TTouch to keep him calm and fully engaged.

How to

Put a headcollar on your donkey and take the lead line in both hands. Position yourself so that you are to the side and slightly in front of him, but avoid overcrowding him. Invite your donkey to walk forwards for a

few steps, then ask him to halt by turning slightly in to face him at an angle as you bring your outside hand around in front of him to touch him gently on the chest. You can add the verbal command 'And whoa' and give a gentle ask-and-release signal on the lead line with your nearest hand if necessary.

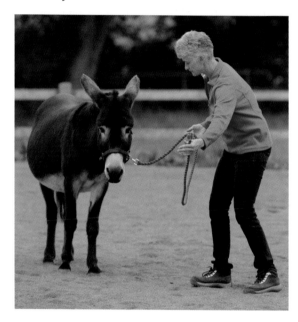

Angle your body towards your donkey and use your outside hand to give a visual signal to halt.

Once he has come to a halt, praise him. If he moves, try calmly bringing him back to a halt and when he understand the visual cue, add a verbal command such as 'Stand'. If you are working with more than one donkey and have the assistance of a friend, remember to ask the second handler to halt the other donkey. It is unfair to ask a fidgety donkey to stand if he thinks his friend is going to disappear or have first dibs on the fodder that may be waiting.

Remember to work in tiny increments. As your donkey begins to process the concept of standing on a cue, you can gradually lengthen the time that you ask him to stay still. If he continues to struggle with the exercise, try using a wand as described in the following exercise.

51. Introducing the wand when working in-hand

Donkeys carry approximately 60 per cent of their bodyweight over their forequarters and many are taught to lead and stop purely from signals on their head. Using a wand when leading can help a donkey learn how to organize his body more efficiently when moving forwards, turning or slowing down, without the need to apply any pressure on the line.

The wand can also be used to increase body awareness and to teach a donkey to halt and stand in balance. If your donkey is alarmed by something in the environment when working in-hand, you can stroke him with the schooling stick to help him settle.

This simple but effective exercise can also help a donkey to become more confident if anything touches him when out and about, and is a useful preparation step for loading.

Considerations

While it can be useful to acquaint your donkey with the wand as described in section 8, some donkeys may find it easier to accept the presence of a schooling stick while they are being led. This exercise can therefore offer a more practical starting point. If you do decide that this is a more favourable option for your donkey, break the steps down into several small sessions.

How to

Hold the line as described in section 47. If you are leading your donkey from his near side, hold the wand and the end of the line in your left hand. If you are leading your donkey from

the off side, have the wand in your right hand. Remember that the wand is an extension of your arm and is there to guide the donkey as well as stroke him.

Stand to the side and slightly in front of your donkey's nose. If you are parallel to his shoulder you may pull him back and out of balance, particularly if he is forward-going. Maintain a light connection with the lead line, and keep your left hand slightly forwards. Angle the wand so that it is in front of the donkey, but 'open', as shown in the photograph. If you hold the wand directly in front of his face you will inhibit forward movement. Keep it low if your donkey

Keep the wand at an angle rather than holding it directly in front of the donkey's nose or chest unless you want him to slow and stop.

shows concern. Move your feet and ask your donkey to step forwards. If the novelty of the situation makes him hesitant, turn him slightly away from you, or towards you, to encourage him to move his front legs.

Walk forwards a few paces, and slowly move the wand towards his chest to slow him down and ultimately halt. Give clear verbal cues such as 'and walk', 'and whoa' so that he starts to learn the association between your voice and his actions. Remember to praise him so he understands what is being asked of him.

Pause for a moment and hold the wand a few inches away from his chest. If you are relaxed and your hand is not tightly gripping the wand, you should feel a connection between the donkey and the schooling stick even though it is not in direct contact with his body. Draw the wand forwards again and out at a slight angle and if necessary give him a gentle signal with the lead line to encourage him to walk.

Repeat this a few times. If he is comfortable with the sight of the moving wand, move it closer towards him to encourage him to slow, and when he halts, stroke him gently down his chest and front limbs. This can help him to maintain the stand.

Extend this exercise over several sessions if necessary until you can stroke him all over his body with the wand when he is standing.

If your donkey is worried about the wand, avoid touching him at first and simply use the schooling stick to help direct him and slow him down. You can also turn it round so that the button end is pointing outwards. This will shorten the amount of stick that the donkey can see and will help him learn that the presence of the wand is nothing to fear.

Remember to switch sides and pay attention to his nervous system responses at all times. You may find that your donkey is quite confident when led and stroked with the wand when you handle him from his near side but becomes anxious or less confident when you repeat the exercise on his off side.

If your donkey cannot move at all, dispense with the wand altogether and use your outside arm to slowly encourage him forwards and to slow him down. Gradually build up this exercise using a small thin branch, then a short riding crop or show cane before trying again with the button end of the wand.

52. Using the wand to teach a straight halt

Teaching a straight halt is not just beneficial for donkeys that compete in-hand, under saddle or when driven. Standing with the weight equally distributed through each limb will help improve balance and proprioception, and promote even muscle development.

Postural traits are formed at an early age and a donkey that habitually rests a leg or stands with one limb forwards, backwards or out to one side may struggle to travel or stand on three legs for the farrier or when his feet are picked out.

Considerations

Always remember that you might be asking a donkey to change a habit that may be deeply entrenched. Think about the way you might cross your legs when sitting down without being fully aware of what you do and then try to sit without crossing your legs or crossing them the other way. Note how frequently you default to your original postural habit throughout the day. Be mindful that your donkey may also have learned to organize his legs in such a way to compensate for discomfort or stiffness somewhere in his body that might need to be addressed.

How to

Hold the lead line and wand in your outside hand and position yourself slightly in front of your donkey's nose but out to the side. Walk him through some of the ground-work exercises or lead him in a shallow serpentine (*see* section 49) to improve proprioception and flexibility.

Ask him to slow by bringing the schooling stick towards him as described in the previous section. As he starts to slow, step ahead and forwards to face your donkey but remain standing to one side. Move the wand towards the opposite front leg as you give an ask-and-release signal on the line and the verbal cue 'and whoa'. The movement of the wand towards the foreleg furthest from you and your own body position will help to keep him straight.

Move the wand towards the donkey's chest and teach the halt between two poles if your donkey finds it difficult to stand straight.

Give the donkey a moment to organize his body. If he is crooked and not standing straight, stroke his legs with the wand to bring awareness to his limbs. Step back away and slightly to the side once more and give a signal with the wand and line to walk forwards.

Alternate between giving a half signal with the wand to slow the donkey down and taking the wand out and at an angle to encourage the donkey to walk out with a longer stride. Always slow him down once more before asking for a halt. Note whether the halt becomes straighter each time.

Keep the sessions short. If he continues to struggle when you practise this exercise again, incorporate body-work such as rocking the withers and/or rocking the back, and use ground-work exercises such as the labyrinth or zigzag poles to help him learn to organize his body more effectively.

53. Using the wand to teach the donkey to step forwards from a signal on the croup

Once a donkey can be stroked all over his body with the dressage schooling stick and is happily walking alongside you, slowing down and halting while you carry it in your hand, you can extend the repertoire of signals you give him with the wand to advance his education.

An unsure donkey may be reluctant to step forwards. He may plant when asked to enter a trailer or his stable, or become stuck when being worked in-hand. Some donkeys also find it hard to stand still. Rather than pulling on his head and triggering the opposition reflex, or applying unnecessary pressure on the sensitive poll joint area, you can teach him to step forwards from a quiet signal on the croup.

This exercise, known as the TTouch Dingo leading position, is also useful for teaching a donkey to tie if he has the habit of pulling back, as a way of improving hind limb engagement and coordination, to help encourage focus and patience, and as a practical foundation step for animals that will go on to be trained in harness or under saddle.

Considerations

Keep your fingers soft and your hand slightly open. If you grip the wand the signal will be harder and potentially unpleasant. If your hand is relaxed, the wand will bounce on your donkey's croup rather than flick and sting. The aim is to improve the donkey's confidence and balance, and encourage him to step forwards on a quiet cue, as opposed to forcing him forwards through fear of being whipped.

How to

This requires a little more skill on the part of the handler as you need to be able to change the way you hold the lead line and wand as well as the position of your body. It is well worth practising, however, as this exercise has proved invaluable over the years.

Ask the donkey to halt if he is in motion and transfer the wand to your hand nearest the donkey. If you are leading him from his near side, this will be your right hand. Fold the length of the lead line across your left hand. Ensure that you do not wrap any part of the line around your hand.

Support your donkey's head by holding the line near his headcollar with your left hand.

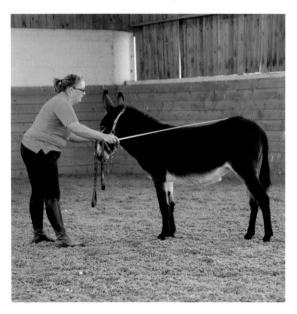

Move your body as you gently stroke the wand along the donkey's back from the withers to the hindquarters.

Remember to keep your connection light, and avoid pulling your donkey's head down or round as this will inhibit his ability to step forwards in balance and in a straight line.

Steady your donkey with your left hand, and stroke him down his front legs if necessary to ensure he is comfortable with the wand. Stroke him along his back with the schooling stick two or three times from just behind his withers to the lumbar region. Give a light ask-and-release signal to walk on with the rope or line and make a forward scooping movement with the wand on your donkey's croup. Give the voice cue 'and walk' as you ask him to move.

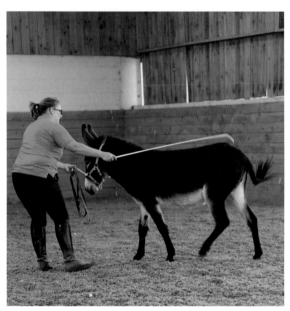

Move your feet as you give a gentle forward signal with the wand and 'scoop the croup'.

If he steps forwards when you stroke him along his back, bring the wand around to the front and stroke him down his chest and forelegs. The idea is to teach him to move when he feels the signal on the croup and line, and not when something touches him on the back. Repeat the smooth strokes along his back and scoop the croup once more.

You can only ask your donkey to step forwards a couple of paces while you are in this leading position. To ask him to halt, bring the wand back around to the front and give an ask-and- release signal on the line. Repeat the exercise or go back to your original leading position, taking the wand in your outside hand and holding the lead line in both hands once again.

54. Using the wand to teach a step back

Stepping back requires engagement of core muscles and hind limbs, good body awareness and a transfer of the centre of gravity. Some donkeys may have only been taught to rein back from the bit or headcollar and will never have learnt to organize their body. Young and unbalanced donkeys often struggle to move backwards in a straight line.

As well as being a useful exercise to teach a donkey in-hand, it can form the basis of educating the donkey to step back on a verbal cue when you are entering the stable or opening a gate. The ability to step backwards in balance is important when asking a donkey to back off a trailer ramp.

Some donkeys that have moved consistently on the forehand for a while can become sore or blocked through the pectoral muscles, and this exercise offers a safe alternative to teaching a step back using your hand to touch them on the chest.

Even if you have already taught your donkey to step back on a verbal cue, it is worth teaching this exercise with the wand. If your donkey becomes stuck on the loading ramp, for example, and you want to back him off before asking him to step into the trailer once more, or if he has become anxious when being led in-

hand, he may not be able to hear and process what you are asking him to do if you only use your voice.

Considerations

Being aware of your own posture and body position will enable you to be more effective with the wand and lead line. Remember that you know what you want to teach your donkey but he doesn't have a clue.

As with all the exercises, you need to give him time to process the signal and organize his body accordingly. You may be asking him to engage muscles that haven't been used effectively for quite some time, so avoid the

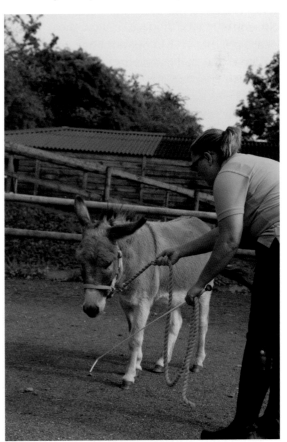

Use the wand to stroke the fore limb and then the diagonal hind limb to encourage your donkey to step back.

temptation to keep repeating the lesson if he is struggling to coordinate his body at first. Build slowly and mix it in with other body-work and leading exercises to improve his balance and proprioception over time.

How to

Hold the lead line and wand as described in section 53. Stand up by your donkey's nose and angle your body towards him. Steady him by holding the lead line up near his headcollar and stroke him gently down the chest and the front of his forelegs with the wand. Continue stroking him along his belly and down the front of his hind limbs.

Avoid pulling on the lead line as you stroke him with the schooling stick. Allow the movement to come from your body and not just your arm. Note which hind leg he needs to move in order to step backwards and stroke that leg and the diagonal foreleg as you transfer your own weight forwards. If he needs to move a fore limb first, stroke the front leg and then the diagonal hind limb. Give him an ask-and-release signal on the line. Note whether he puts one leg out to the side, swings his body in one direction or leans forward into the headcollar. If he struggles, go back to an exercise he found easier and then ask again.

If he continues to struggle, try teaching him to back up using the Balance Rein or the back-up exercise with the hand.

55. Using your hand to teach a step back

This exercise has similar practical applications to those described in the section on teaching a step back with the wand. If your donkey is comfortable with contact on his chest, he may find this exercise easier to understand than teaching him to step back with a schooling stick, as you are actively showing him how to organize his body in order to move effectively.

Considerations

If your donkey is weak through the top line and hindquarters or has changes to the skeleton due to injury or disease, avoid asking him to step back unless he readily offers the behaviour. If he is really sensitive to contact on the chest, use the body-work exercises listed in the section covering the withers, chest and shoulders to help address his concerns.

How to

Stand to one side of your donkey's head and observe his posture. If he is unlevel and has the majority of his weight on his near hind, or is standing with his off hind further forward for example, place the palm of your hand on the near side of his chest. If you think he will need to move the left hind leg in order to move backwards, place your hand on the right side of his chest.

If you are standing on his left side, use your left hand. Start with your weight on your back foot and slowly transfer your weight forwards onto your front foot.

Imagine that you are supporting the end of an invisible line with your hand and that you are going to glide the line up through his body from his chest at an angle so that it activates his diagonal hind limb. As he takes a step back, slowly release your hand.

Switch sides and give him the same signal on the other side of his chest to step back with the opposite hind limb. The movement through your donkey's body should come from the transfer of your own weight onto your front foot. Avoid too many repetitions in one go.

Once your donkey is able to step back effortlessly each time, add the voice cue 'and back' as you give the signal on his chest. Lighten the signal as you progress over several

Note which hind leg your donkey needs to move to step back from a signal on his chest.

Use your own body and give him an ask-and-release signal on the diagonal shoulder to encourage him to move his hind leg.

sessions if necessary until your donkey is able to step back from the slightest touch.

You can add the voice cue earlier if you choose but remember the donkey will need time to learn the association between the action and the word. It may be easier for him to understand what you are saying if you teach the movement first.

56. Walk over poles

Teaching a donkey to walk over poles forms an important part of his education. It teaches him to remain calm if he comes across an obstacle in his path and can help improve balance, proprioception and self-control. It

also provides a simple foundation step for teaching a donkey to load or step on to a weigh bridge and for more complex pole work later on. It can also be of benefit for donkeys that worry when their hooves are picked out or trimmed.

Considerations

Ensure you select poles that are a suitable height for your donkey. If he has arthritis in his joints, he may struggle to lift his legs. You can use lengths of hosepipe or half-round rails if a standard jump pole is too big for a little donkey or too challenging for a donkey with reduced mobility through his limbs. Regardless of the type of obstacle you choose, ensure that it cannot get caught around your donkey's hooves or break if he steps on it by mistake.

How to

Lay the pole in an area where it is clearly visible and lead your donkey around the pole so that he can become accustomed to the sight of a potentially novel object lying on the ground. Observe your donkey's responses and work at a distance that is acceptable before asking him to walk around each end of the pole.

Practise asking your donkey to walk, slow down and halt using a gentle cue with the wand before you approach the pole. Walk him towards the pole and ask him to stop before inviting him to step over the pole. Ask him to halt on the other side. Rushing and an inability to halt with the pole behind him can indicate your donkey is concerned. Lead him away if he is anxious and ask him to do something he found easy before asking him to walk over the pole once more.

Lead him over the pole from both directions and, if possible, practise leading him from

Walk your donkey towards the pole and ask him to halt. If he rushes over the pole or moves away, he is concerned.

Add more poles or use the labyrinth as walk over poles to improve balance and proprioception.

both sides. Note if he clips the pole with any hoof and see if this is a consistent pattern. If he continually touches the pole, try stroking his legs with the wand before he steps over. See if this helps him to be more aware of his legs and feet. If he continues to struggle, think about ways of simplifying the exercise by teaching him to step over a smaller object instead.

As he grows in confidence, add more poles and vary the complexity of the exercise over several sessions if necessary by raising one end of each pole or alternate poles to improve hoof–eye coordination and encourage greater flexion through his back and limbs.

57. Straddling a pole

Some donkeys that are disconnected from their hind limbs find it hard to stand with their front feet on one side of a pole and their back feet on the other side. Nervous donkeys may also find this exercise rather challenging at first.

This seemingly simple exercise may be difficult to master but it can be a valuable part of a donkey's education. It can be helpful for donkeys that get stuck on the loading ramp and can improve self-carriage, self-confidence and self-control. It also helps handlers to improve observations, awareness and timing.

Considerations

Start by teaching your donkey to walk over a pole or half-rail depending on his size and general mobility. Practise the halt and step back in-hand prior to teaching the donkey to back over the pole.

How to

Start the session by walking your donkey over a single pole. Once he is happy to halt with the pole in front of him and behind him, walk

him towards the pole and ask him to stop with the pole quite close to his forelegs but with enough of a gap that he does not crowd the pole.

Invite him to step over the pole. As he starts to cross the pole with his second foreleg, give a gentle ask-and-release signal on the lead line and bring the wand towards his chest. Use the voice cue 'and whoa'.

The timing and the clarity of your signals are crucial. Remember that your donkey needs time to organize his body and to process what you are asking him to do. If you wait too long to give the cues, your donkey may have already crossed the pole but if you are too quick and your donkey already understands the signals, he may place his second front hoof back on the other side of the pole. Practice makes perfect! The aim is to teach your donkey to stand

Invite your donkey to step over the pole with both front legs, and then ask him to stand.

quietly with both forefeet on one side of the single pole until you invite him to walk right over the pole.

Once you and your donkey have mastered the art of straddling the pole, you can ask him to step back so that he must lift his front feet over the pole while moving backwards. Once he is happily backing up, you can progress to teaching your donkey how to back over the pole with his hind legs as well, so that he executes this whole exercise in reverse.

You can further refine this exercise by teaching your donkey to stand in balance with one foreleg over the pole, then one hind leg, so that he learns to straddle the pole first with his forelimbs and then his hind limbs. Note which leg he leads with; if he always stands

with his nearside front leg over the pole and then his offside hind leg, for example, see if you can encourage him to straddle the pole the other way.

58. Random poles

Teaching a donkey to walk over random poles improves hoof–eye coordination as well as balance and confidence.

This exercise can add variety when working in-hand as the layout of the poles can be changed in every session and offers a practical step for helping donkeys negotiate their way over any debris that may be lying on the ground. It can also help to keep a donkey calm

Once your donkey can straddle the pole with both front legs, teach him to place one front foot over the pole. Note whether he struggles to step over with a particular leg.

in an emergency situation, particularly if his legs have become entangled in any broken or fallen fencing.

Considerations

As with other ground-work exercises, make sure the poles you use are an appropriate size for your donkey. Teach your donkey how to step over a single pole before advancing to this part of his education.

How to

It is as simple as it sounds. Gradually add multiple poles in different positions and vary the distances between them to encourage the donkey to focus on the placement of his hooves. Raise some of the ends with Pole Pods or on mini cavaletti blocks to increase the complexity of the exercise in stages and over several sessions if necessary.

Once your donkey can pick his way over a variety of random poles, add the straddling the pole exercise into the mix.

59. Zigzag poles

This exercise helps to encourage the donkey to soften and yield through his neck and body and can improve balance as it teaches the donkey to flex left and right. As the donkey is working between parallel poles, it can also be used to help teach a straight halt.

It is an excellent exercise for donkeys that are initially worried about walking through the labyrinth (*see* section 60), those that are elderly and/or stiff, and those that find it hard to turn in a particular direction. The angles of the poles can be altered to suit each donkey and more poles can be added to increase the length of the exercise.

Considerations

If your donkey is worried by poles on the ground, start with two parallel poles wide apart. Add additional poles either in pairs or one at a time if your donkey is concerned when asked to walk between the poles. Leave spaces between the ends of the poles at first so that your donkey

Using poles to teach your donkey to flex left and right gives him a visual guide and improves focus and balance.

has the option of walking out of the zigzag if necessary. If he does not have a get-out clause, he may rush through the track.

How to

Arrange the poles as shown in the photograph. Attach the lead line or rope to the side of your donkey's headcollar and take the line in both hands. If your donkey is habituated to being handled from the near side, start by leading him from his left side. Position yourself by your donkey's nose so that you can guide him around the turns. Keep your hips and knees soft and allow the movement to come from your feet and up into the lead line. If you brace through the shoulders and try to push or pull your donkey around the turns he may stop, pull back or rush.

As you zigzag your donkey through the turns, note whether it is easier for him to turn in a particular direction, whether he tilts his head when flexing his neck, gets stuck, speeds up or walks into you. The aim of the exercise is to teach him to maintain the same distance from you regardless of the direction of the turn.

Once he has happily walked through the poles once, repeat the exercise but ask him to halt just before each turn. Remember to lead him from both sides and ask him to walk through the zigzag from both directions. Increase the angle as you progress so that each turn encourages more flexibility, and narrow the distance between the poles. When your donkey is comfortable walking through a narrow track, ask him to walk through the pattern of poles while you remain on the outside of the track.

60. Labyrinth

The labyrinth is a pattern of poles arranged in a specific manner. It is a fundamental TTouch ground-work exercise and has been instrumental in helping animals overcome a wide range of problems. It is a natural progression from the zigzag exercise but can also be used on its own.

The simplicity of this exercise belies the value that it offers. Leading a donkey through the poles helps improve balance, proprioception and hind limb engagement, and increases self-confidence and self-control.

It can have an incredibly calming effect on even the most fractious equine, and can give you a greater understanding of a donkey's ability to accept any new equipment. If a donkey has not truly processed the sensation of wearing a saddle, for example, he might not be able to negotiate the turns through the labyrinth even though he may appear to walk happily in a circle or straight line.

The labyrinth also improves flexibility and can help the donkey release habitual patterns of bracing in just two or three repetitions. If you only have space to set up one ground-work exercise, use the labyrinth or create one on the route out to your donkey's field if you want to help your donkey but are short of time.

Considerations

Start with the poles fairly wide apart if your donkey is nervous, elderly, young or stiff. It is important to halt before the end of each pole to maximize the effectiveness of this exercise. Leave gaps between the poles so that you have the option to walk your donkey out of the labyrinth if he becomes stuck or overwhelmed.

How to

Lead your donkey through the labyrinth from his near side initially. Hold the wand and the end of the lead in your left hand and support the line in your right hand, palm up, by the headcollar. Stay just ahead of your donkey's nose. Remember to use the wand as an extension of your arm or just use your arm if you do not want to carry a wand.

Ask your donkey to halt just before the end of each pole. Give him time to listen to your signal and then organize his body. Keep your feet moving until he stops to avoid pulling him off or around to one side. If he is nervous and cannot flex or stop, lead him quietly out of the labyrinth or let him step over the outside pole and try again.

Pay attention to the way he moves his hind limbs on each turn. Can he flex relatively evenly left and right or does he swivel his body round and straddle the internal pole? Note how light or braced and heavy he feels in the hand. If your donkey is stiff or the poles are too narrow, you may need to step outside the labyrinth to give him room to turn.

Ask your donkey to halt between the parallel poles before inviting him to turn. Keep the line loose and stay in front of your donkey's nose to help guide him around the bend.

Once your donkey has mastered the art of halting and turning through the labyrinth while being led, try working at liberty using your arms and body position to give the signals to walk forwards, bend and halt.

Remember to lead him through the poles from both ends and from both sides if possible. Vary the sessions by using the labyrinth as walk-over poles, or by placing different surfaces between the poles. You can also add novel shapes outside the labyrinth. Your donkey will probably settle more quickly when you combine the introduction of unfamiliar items with a ground-work exercise that he already knows.

61. Sliding saddle pad

Teaching a donkey to calmly halt, instead of rushing forwards, when he feels something falling from his back is a valuable exercise for any donkey that will be ridden or taught to carry a pack. It also helps to keep a donkey settled when you are rugging up or adjusting

rugs, or when introducing new equipment that may be unfamiliar to the donkey.

Considerations

If your donkey is really food motivated, try using something of lower value than sweet tasty treats. Many donkeys will work quite happily for small amounts of hay. Ensure your donkey fully processes each step of the exercise and is not simply focusing on the food.

How to

You will need a light cloth pad, a helper and some food. Ask your helper to practise walking and halting the donkey on cue. Walk next to your donkey holding the cloth or pad in your hand. If he remains relaxed, place the cloth

Walk the donkey forwards while your assistant holds the saddle pad in place before gently sliding it from your donkey's back.

on his back when he comes to a halt. Remain on the same side as the handler at all times.

Ask your helper to invite your donkey to walk forwards. Let him walk for a few strides then gently slide the cloth from his back as he is moving and ask your donkey to halt using the verbal cue 'and whoa'. If your donkey cannot stop, ask your helper to give him a gentle signal with the lead line. If he continues to move, he may be worried or unsure.

Lay the cloth on the ground and place the food rewards on the material. Encourage your donkey to turn and take the treat if he does not automatically choose to explore the pad. Ensure your donkey does not make a grab for the food and pick the cloth up by mistake.

Repeat this part of the exercise three or four times before you and the handler switch sides. Work through the steps from the other side until your donkey is happily halting the moment he feels the cloth 'falling' from his back. If he offers a halt the moment you touch the cloth, encourage him forwards until the pad actually starts to slide.

Vary the rewards and alternate between verbal praise and a gentle scratch as well as food so that the donkey does not become frustrated if treats do not appear if he ever feels a pack, saddle or person sliding from his back.

Extend this exercise further by sliding the saddle cloth over your donkey's hindquarters and tail. If there is any risk that your donkey will kick out, work through the body-work tips for releasing tension in his hindquarters and tail before moving on to this part of the exercise.

Step back so that the donkey can easily access the treats on the pad. Avoid ending up on the opposite side from your assistant.

on the ground. Even if you have introduced various textures to the donkey's environment, teaching them to walk over different surfaces on a cue is different and can help develop greater confidence and trust.

This exercise has many practical applications for all donkeys but is of particular importance for donkeys that go out and about, whether they are to be ridden, driven, shown in-hand or attend fêtes. This exercise is also an important foundation step for loading and for teaching donkeys to walk onto a weighbridge.

62. Walking over different surfaces

Many donkeys are naturally wary about stepping onto or over a novel surface or object

Considerations
Remember that the donkey has to become accustomed to the sight of the surface, the noise it makes when it is stepped on, and the

sensation of the different textures under his feet. Donkeys like to use their noses to explore novel items, so it is likely that your donkey will sniff the different surface and may even test it with his teeth. Avoid letting him nibble the surface if it is something that he can pick up with his mouth. If he becomes worried, he may not be able to release the surface and may rocket backwards with it still held firmly in his mouth, which will naturally alarm him even more.

Avoid using anything that can move or flap if working in windy weather. Carpet squares, car or door mats, lengths of rubber matting and flat solid boards are useful surfaces that can be used.

How to

Set up a labyrinth or an exercise that the donkey knows well if possible and place the novel surface near the pattern of poles. This gives you the option of starting with, and returning to, a familiar exercise if the donkey becomes concerned.

If you do not have sufficient room or appropriate equipment for a pole work exercise, lay the surface on the ground and ensure that there is enough space for you to walk your donkey around the mat or carpet so that he can become accustomed to the sight of the object before you ask him to step onto or walk over it. If your donkey is worried by unfamiliar objects on the ground, ask him to follow a more confident friend.

Allow him time to gather information about the surface you are using by letting him sniff it or test it with one hoof. Build in small steps by halting him in front of the mat or carpet square before asking him to step onto it. If he rushes or cannot stop on the other side, he is concerned.

Give your donkey as much time as he needs to explore the different surfaces.

Keep the lead line loose and let your donkey find his own way over the surfaces so that he always has a choice.

Avoid forcing him to walk over the surface. If you give him time to process what you are asking him to do and build the trust between you, the more readily and more calmly he will be able to step onto and eventually stand on the item.

If he continues to struggle, try placing the surface between two poles (provided you have taught the zigzag exercise first). This can help to give him more visual information and keep him balanced, focused and engaged.

Some donkeys may settle more quickly if there is more than one novel item to work around, and you can gradually bring them together as described in the walking over plastic sheeting exercise, but others may appreciate the opportunity to get used to a single object first.

63. Walking over plastic sheeting

Teaching a donkey to walk over plastic sheeting has many practical applications. It provides a foundation exercise for teaching donkeys to walk through water and to remain calm if there is any movement or noise from coloured bunting, tent flaps or blowing litter at a fete or show.

This exercise also helps build confidence in donkeys that are worried by the rustling of waterproof clothing worn by their handler or passers-by and adds another new experience for all donkeys whether they will be staying at home or venturing out and about.

Considerations

You will need two lengths of plastic sheeting or soft plastic water trays. You will also need a helper to move the plastic for you if possible as you will not be able to move the plastic while holding on to your donkey.

Ideally, this exercise is best taught in an indoor arena, barn or on a calm day. If you do not have access to a sheltered area, use jump poles to weigh down the plastic sheets to ensure they don't flap about or move in the wind. If you have an assistant, make sure they move the sheeting slowly and that your donkey is able to watch from a safe distance. If you do not have a helper on hand, pop your donkey back in his stable before you narrow the gap between the sheets.

If you are working in an arena, be aware that your feet or your donkey's hooves may flick the surface of the school on to the plastic, which might alarm your donkey if you are progressing too quickly.

How to

Lay two sheets of plastic on the ground in an open-ended arrowhead as shown. Lead your donkey around the plastic so that he has a good opportunity to observe the surfaces from a distance that he finds acceptable. If he freezes, lifts his head or shows other signs of concern, give him a moment to process the visual information and try stroking him down his chest and front limbs with the wand to help him settle and engage, or give him a gentle scratch behind his withers.

Once he can walk quietly past the plastic, ask him to halt in front of the widest point of the arrowhead. Invite him to walk slowly through the gap between the plastic sheets. Pay attention to his speed as this will give you valuable information about his levels of confidence or concern.

Repeat this step and ask him to halt on the other side of the arrow head. If he cannot stop, it will indicate that he is worried. Go back a step and let him walk straight through the gap, widen the space between the sheets or lead him around the outside of the plastic before trying again.

Ask your donkey to halt midway between the sheets but make sure that he is able to stand quietly without using a strong signal on the lead line. If he cannot halt with confidence, he may swing his quarters around and step on the plastic, which might worry him even more.

Stroke the donkey down his chest and front legs with the wand and let him look at the plastic. If he wants to sniff the plastic ensure he doesn't pick it up with his teeth. Continue on through the arrowhead and ask him to stop on the other side. Remember to pay attention to his body language, including any quickening of pace, and avoid the temptation to rush through any of the steps.

Once your donkey can walk calmly between the two pieces of plastic and is able to halt and

Start with an open arrowhead and allow your donkey time to observe the plastic sheeting from a distance that is comfortable for him.

wait for a forward cue in front of, in the middle and at the end of the arrowhead, lead him through again but walk on the plastic yourself so that you can accustom your donkey to the noise of feet on the sheeting. He needs to hear the sound before he feels the texture under his hooves. Breaking any learning down as much as possible will give your donkey the opportunity to process each small step and give you valuable information as to which part of the exercise might be causing some concern.

Quietly lead him through the open arrowhead. Observe the position of his ears as he passes the plastic.

Narrow the arrowhead a little and lead your donkey through the plastic sheets again, repeating the earlier steps. Remember to put your donkey back in his stable before moving the sheeting if you are working on your own.

Gradually continue bringing the ends of the plastic closer and closer together, repeating the exercise each time until the ends of the sheeting meet. This offers the donkey the opportunity

Gradually decrease the space between the ends of the plastic until your donkey is able to calmly step over the sheeting at its narrowest point.

to walk over a short length of plastic and helps to build his confidence in small steps.

Once your donkey is happily crossing the plastic at the end of the set up, you can invite him to walk across the plastic arrowhead widthways and finally up the length of one sheet.

You can vary the exercise by asking your donkey to step onto the plastic and halt, and then ask him to calmly back away.

64. Walking through puddles

Many equids avoid walking through water and donkeys will generally neatly sidestep puddles or rush through muddy patches if they cannot be avoided.

Teaching a donkey to walk through water on a cue has beneficial applications as it helps to slow down a fast-moving donkey that may try to jump over water that has collected in the yard or gateway. It teaches a donkey to stay calm if the route to his stable is blocked by shallow water following a sudden downpour or small flood.

Any donkey that will be going out and about will benefit from learning that walking through puddles is nothing to fear as swerving to avoid surface water can be dangerous if the donkey is being ridden or driven on a road.

Considerations

Asking an animal to engage in an activity that it instinctively would prefer to avoid requires trust and understanding. Forcing an animal to face his fears can break down the human/animal bond and exacerbate that fear. Many equines quickly overcome a fear of water when they learn to walk over plastic sheeting so it is well worth teaching that exercise first. As with all the exercises, break it down into small steps and remember to give plenty of praise and breaks.

If you have already taught your donkey to follow the cues from a dressage schooling stick when working in-hand, you may find it easier to keep him calm and fully engaged. You can use the wand to stroke his legs and body to keep him relaxed, and encourage him to move forwards or to back away.

How to

Set up two soft plastic water trays in the same formation as the sheeting in the 'walking over plastic' exercise. If you cannot locate water trays, try using rubber car mats or something similar that offers a non-slip surface with indentations that you can fill with a little water. You can also create a shallow tray using plastic sheeting with the edges rolled up to hold the water, but be sure to place a non-slip surface such as thin rubber matting inside. You could also use flat, wide rubber feeding bowls provided you have already taught your donkey to step into the empty container.

Teach your donkey to step onto and then stand on whatever object you are using without adding water. Ask a helper to sprinkle some water onto the surface or put your donkey in

Teach your donkey to walk along a plastic tray or step into a container before adding water.

his stable while you add some water to the tray or mat. Remember that the set-up will now look, feel, smell and sound a little different and your donkey will need time to process the new sensory information.

Add more water in stages until there is a reasonable covering. If the water is going to splash when the donkey puts his hooves in the puddle, you should walk through the water first so that he can hear the noise from your own feet.

If he is really worried and cannot step into the water when asked, dampen a soft sponge that you have already used to touch your donkey (*see* section 9) and break down the exercise further by doing TTouches around the coronary band and hoof wall. Gradually make the sponge wetter so that water trickles over his feet.

Practise this exercise in different locations around your property or utilize natural puddles as they appear.

65. Walking through a 'rubbish pit'

Teaching a donkey to negotiate 'debris' on the ground follows on from teaching him to walk over random poles, through puddles, through patterns of poles and across different surfaces. It builds confidence in donkeys that will be venturing out and about and attending shows and events.

Considerations

Use items that are safe, will not blow around if you are working outside in windy weather or injure the donkey if he treads on them by mistake.

How to

Lay jump poles in a square so that you create a box and lead your donkey over the poles from all directions. Ask him to halt in the middle of the square, then walk him out.

Ask a helper to place your first item in one corner of the box and walk your donkey around the outside of the poles so that he has a chance to observe the new addition at a distance he deems safe. Then walk him through the square. Gradually add more items in random positions as you progress, observing his reactions at all times.

66. Stepping onto a raised platform

Donkeys love to succeed, just like us, and they benefit from simple, logical steps in their education. Teaching them to stand with their front feet on a solid block and then walk over the platform gives them the opportunity to learn a new skill and helps them to develop trust and confidence.

This is a progression from section 62 and can form a useful foundation for loading for donkeys that are worried when asked to step onto a weighbridge or the trailer ramp.

Considerations

Ensure that the block or platform you are using is safe, stable and solid, and that there is sufficient room for your donkey to move around the block when you first introduce this exercise. Avoid anything that might be slippery or break, and make sure there are no gaps or sharp edges on the platform that could catch the donkey's hoof.

How to

If it is easy to move, place your block in the centre of the area where you are working and allow your donkey to walk around it before inviting him to stand anywhere near the block. Observe his reactions and give him time to process the new object.

Remember to give your donkey the chance to explore the raised platform with his nose (and hooves) if necessary.

Lead him towards the block and ask him to halt in front of the obstacle at a distance that is comfortable for him. Stroke him down his chest and front legs with the wand or along his neck with the back of your hand. With the wand give him the signal to walk forwards towards the block.

Let your donkey explore the block with his hooves or muzzle, and drop some grass or small treats onto it if appropriate. Quietly walk him away from the block or ask him to back up. Reminding a nervous donkey that he can back away quietly from something novel can help improve his confidence and override the need to spin or move away at speed.

Walk your donkey towards the block once more and this time stand on the block yourself so that the donkey has the opportunity to hear the sound of your feet on the box before he puts his front feet on the block. Remember that you will also appear taller, so keep your posture low at first and if your donkey is concerned only gradually stand up. If you step quickly onto the block you will not know if it is the change in your body posture or the noise that is causing any alarm.

Step off and lead your donkey around before inviting him to place his front feet on the block. Avoid the temptation to lure or pull him onto the platform. If you have practised pole work and working on different surfaces, he will quickly get the idea. Ask him to back off and then walk him forwards again and over the block.

Remember to praise him at every opportunity.

67. Walking through narrow spaces

Teaching a donkey to walk through narrow spaces helps to improve spatial awareness and can be beneficial for donkeys that rush through gateways or stable doors. It provides a useful starting point for donkeys that struggle to walk onto a weighbridge or into a trailer, and is a foundation exercise for donkeys that will go

Allow him to sniff the surface as he walks over the boards if that is what he wants to do.

on to be ridden, driven or competed in-hand and for those that will be attending fêtes and events.

Considerations

As with all the exercises, think about how you can break this ground-work down into small steps so that your donkey can develop confidence and trust. Ensure that any objects you use such as jump fillers, blocks or bales of straw or bedding are stable and safe if your donkey wants to explore them with his nose. If he is really worried when asked to walk between two obstacles, start by teaching the zigzag or labyrinth ground-work exercises.

Remember that you may be introducing new items to your donkey or changing the context of something familiar by asking him to walk between two objects as opposed to walking past them or by altering the location of an obstacle that he already knows. Always work at his pace and build the exercise over time.

When introducing a new exercise, it is always

worth setting up something that the donkey already knows, such as a labyrinth or even a single pole. If he struggles with any new element at any point, you can return to the exercise that is more familiar before you ask him to try the potentially more complex task.

How to

Start with one obstacle and work at a distance that is comfortable and safe for your donkey. Ask him to approach the object from both sides and teach him to stand parallel to, and in front of, the obstacle before adding another.

Ensure there is plenty of space between the two objects and ask him to halt before you lead him through the gap. Remember to lead him through from both directions. Pay attention to any reluctance to walk forwards or a quickening of his pace that might indicate your donkey is concerned. Ask him to halt once he has walked through the gap. If your donkey cannot stand still with the barriers or blocks behind him, or if he swings his hindquarters either away from

Walk your donkey around and then towards the obstacles while they are fairly wide apart.

Gradually decrease the space between the obstacles and extend the length of the corridor over several sessions if necessary.

you or towards you, he may not be quite as confident with this exercise as you might think.

Progress with the exercise by teaching your donkey to stand between the barriers or blocks before asking him to walk on. Stroke him gently with a wand to help keep him calm and fully engaged. Gradually narrow the gap as your donkey develops more confidence and add more obstacles or vary the items that you are using to give him additional experiences.

68. Introducing a second handler

Teaching a donkey to lead between two people not only habituates him to being led from both sides but can encourage straightness and balance. It teaches the donkey to process information from both sides of the body and is therefore a useful foundation for donkeys that will be ridden or driven.

This TTouch leading exercise, known as the Homing Pigeon, is also useful for introducing a person who may be less familiar to the donkey. It can be incorporated into ground-work that the donkey may already know, thus diffusing the focus from the presence of the person that might be giving the donkey cause for concern.

Considerations

Although two handlers are involved in this exercise, only one person is going to be influencing the donkey at any one time. The second person acts as a neutral support and is there when needed if the donkey requires a little assistance, for example through a turn. In order to avoid giving conflicting signals or confusing the donkey by trying to influence him from both sides at once, clear communication between the handlers is crucial.

If you are working with a really timid donkey or a donkey that may never have been handled from one particular side, use the long sliding

line as described in the section on connecting with novice and nervous donkeys instead of a second fixed lead line. If he panics, the sliding line can be easily removed.

How to

Both handlers can carry wands in this exercise if necessary unless the sliding line is used. They are held in the outside hand along with the end of the lead line, but if this causes the donkey any concern, you can dispense with the second wand. If schooling sticks are not available or appropriate, the handlers can use their outside arms to give the visual cues to the donkey to walk, slow down, turn and halt.

The primary handler will give the signals with the wand and can back up the aid with a light ask-and-release signal on the line if necessary. As with the majority of the in-hand exercises, the aim is to teach the donkey to alter his balance through the transitions at a signal from the wand, rather than from a pull on his head.

To minimize the risk of pulling back on the lead line if the donkey is forward-going, both handlers need to remember to keep their hands forwards.

Start in walk without doing pole work until you are all used to the exercise. Position yourselves slightly forwards, in front of the donkey's nose, so that you can see each other clearly without having to look over the top of the donkey's head or neck. The primary handler can stroke the donkey on the chest and down the front legs with the wand and then draw the wand forwards and out level with his chest to invite the donkey to walk.

If the donkey doesn't understand the exercise or is concerned by the presence of the second handler, the primary leader can repeat the step and give a little ask-and-release signal on the lead line at the same time. If the donkey is stuck and starts to shut down, one of the handlers can stroke the lead line to reconnect with the donkey and help him rebalance before the

Both handlers need to keep the lines free from tension to avoid applying pressure on the donkey's head.

primary handler invites him to walk forwards once again.

The second handler maintains a neutral support on the line and, if carrying a second wand, keeps it forwards. If two wands are used, keep them level with each other with the tips pointing towards each other, without touching, to form an open-ended triangle. If the donkey is bowling on, the primary handler can bring the wand back part-way towards the donkey's chest to slow him down and then open the wand again so that they can repeat the movement if required.

The primary handler needs to give clear instruction to both the donkey and the second handler, particularly when planning a turn or halt.

69. The Bee Line

This is another TTouch leading technique that can be helpful for introducing a second person as it allows the donkey to choose, to a degree, how close he positions himself to the new handler. It also gives the donkey more freedom when being worked in-hand and encourages flexibility through the neck and back.

Many equines that brace and lean into the headcollar or bridle become lighter and are able to move in better balance after one experience of the Bee Line.

Considerations

Clear communication with your assistant is crucial and it is imperative that neither handler pulls back on the line. This exercise is best introduced in a secure area such as an arena or paddock. If the handlers fall behind the donkey's shoulders due to lack of experience and the donkey shoots forwards and cannot slow down, one handler can let go of the rope so that it can be pulled from the headcollar.

How to

You will need one helper and a length of climbing rope, some 6-7m long. Thread the rope through the central ring at the back of the noseband of the headcollar. Decide which handler is going to give the directions to walk, slow and turn. You need a plan when working in-hand so that you know where you want to go but remember to be flexible with the plan as your donkey does not know what you intend to do.

Both handlers need to be parallel with the donkey's nose, or even slightly in front, with their hands low. The rope should be held between both hands and over the palms.

Use your outside hand to give signals to the donkey to walk forwards, slow turn and turn. Ensure that no part of the rope loops over your hand at any time. If the donkey finds it hard to stop or slow, ask your handler to stretch the rope while you do the same, and then release the rope together as the donkey slows or halts. This 'meet and melt' signal will help the donkey balance. Pulling backwards will trigger

The Bee Line encourages a donkey to lower his neck and lengthen his top line.

the opposition reflex and send the donkey forwards.

70. Walking up from behind

Teaching a donkey to turn and look at someone approaching him from behind is a fun and practical exercise. It can help to develop confidence and teaches a donkey to act rather than react should something startle him from behind. It also forms a practical foundation for

helping donkeys overcome a reluctance to be caught.

If you are ever in the unfortunate position of trying to retrieve an escapee who is heading off down a narrow track, you will be thrilled (and very grateful) that you taught him this simple skill.

Considerations

You will need to enlist the help of a friend and some treats. Keep the treats as low value as possible so that the donkey does not become overly pushy around the food. Small amounts of grass or hay generally work really well but some donkeys prefer higher value treats, such as donkey nuts or carrot slices (cut lengthways). Always ensure that the treats are small and cannot choke your donkey if he tries to wolf them down.

Remember to work at your donkey's pace and over several small sessions if he is really anxious. Always ensure that you and your second handler work from the same side. It is imperative that your donkey has a get-out clause at all times and does not feel trapped.

Ask your assistant to walk behind the donkey but out to the side so that the donkey can see them in his peripheral vision.

Reward the donkey for halting with a little treat when you start teaching this exercise.

If you need to change direction, ensure that you and your assistant remain on the inside of the turn.

How to

Lead your donkey and ask him to halt and walk on with your verbal cues. If your donkey is calm and settled, ask your assistant to walk behind him at a safe distance but out to the side so that your donkey can see them in his peripheral vision. If your donkey quickens his pace, stops and raises his head, or spins around to watch your assistant, he is concerned.

Ask your helper to give the cue 'and whoa'. Remember the context has changed and your donkey may not be able to process the verbal cue from a different person, or from a different location. If he keeps walking forwards, you can give him a visual cue with your outside hand and a gentle ask-and-release signal on the lead line.

Ask your assistant to walk up to the side of the donkey and offer him a treat. When he has eaten his reward, invite your donkey to walk forwards once again. Your assistant should fall back so that you can repeat the exercise a few times. Your donkey should quickly learn to listen to your assistant and to stop when he hears them give the verbal cue.

If he starts to anticipate the offering of a treat, encourage the donkey to keep moving until he is actually asked to halt. It is important that he does not learn to stop every time he sees someone walking up behind him.

The aim is to teach your donkey to turn his head rather than swing his entire body

The outside hand is the active hand and gives an ask-and-release signal upwards while your inside hand supports the Balance Rein.

remains calm if someone ever approaches him from behind at a quicker pace.

71. Using the Balance Rein in-hand

Teaching a donkey to slow down and halt from a signal round the neck can help improve balance. It teaches him how to organize his body more effectively and can encourage him to lift through the withers and lengthen, and ultimately to strengthen his top line.

It provides a useful foundation step for ridden work and chest line driving, and gives all donkeys a new experience whether they have poor balance or not.

round when he hears the cue, and to remain stationary until he is given the signal to walk on once more. Teach the exercise from both sides and build over several sessions if necessary.

Once your donkey is consistently able to stop when led and approached from both sides, start to fade out the treats and use verbal praise or a gentle scratch instead. You can extend this exercise and ask your assistant to run up slowly at first, then a little faster, so that your donkey

Considerations

If your donkey is particularly stiff or shows signs of discomfort around his chest, start with the Half Wrap as described in section 45. You will need a helper and a length of relatively wide rope, or you can buy a TTEAM Balance Rein online. If you do not have access to either a Balance Rein or a length of rope, cut the clip off a regular lead rope and use that instead. (If you leave the clip attached, you may catch your fingers in the hook or bang the donkey with the snap if you have to let go of the rope.)

Ensure that the equipment you use is not too narrow or flat like a neck strap. You can give a clearer but more subtle signal with a round, relatively wide rope.

How to

Ask your helper to lead your donkey while you walk parallel to his shoulder. Ensure that you remain on the same side as your assistant at all times. If you are walking on a circle keep to the inside for safety reasons and to avoid having to quicken your pace if your donkey speeds up on the turns. You may need to keep reminding your assistant to stay ahead of the donkey's nose. If they walk too slowly or fall back behind the donkey's head, you will probably trip over or step on their feet.

Ask your handler to invite your donkey to slow down and halt a few times using a voice cue and a signal on the line or with the wand as appropriate. Once your donkey is happily walking, slowing and halting with you by his shoulder, place the Balance Rein around the base of his neck.

With your hand nearest the donkey, hold one end of the rope over or near his withers and take the other end of the rope in your outside hand. The outside hand will be the active hand. If you are starting this exercise on your donkey's near side, you will be holding the end of the rope in your left hand, while your right hand maintains the connection.

Keep the rope slack but without dropping it down so low that it impedes any movement through the donkey's chest or front legs. Ask your handler to give the cue 'and whoa' and, as the donkey starts to slow down, give a gentle ask-and-release signal with your left hand by moving the rope in an upwards direction, following the line of his shoulder. Keep your right hand still and quiet and avoid pulling the donkey towards you by bringing

either or both hands inadvertently out to the side.

The donkey should feel the signal on the base of his neck near his chest. Avoid maintaining a pull on the Balance Rein as this will encourage the donkey to lean into the connection and walk on or speed up. It is on the release that the donkey will slow down and halt. If he stops, remember to praise him and release the connection before asking him to walk forwards once more. Once he understands the exercise, you can start giving him the voice cues to walk forwards, slow down and halt, as opposed to your handler giving all the verbal commands.

You may need to repeat the steps a few times before the donkey learns how to stop on the rope signal, as this may be a totally new experience for him. Once he is happily walking, slowing and halting from one side, introduce the exercise on his less familiar side and remember to ask your assistant to change sides too.

72. Chest line driving

This is a natural progression from the Balance Rein and can help improve balance, self-carriage and self-confidence. It offers a fun way to advance your donkey's education and can help them learn that movement behind them is nothing to fear.

Chest line driving encourages donkeys to walk forward in balance and is a useful exercise for donkeys that find it hard to slow down when led. It also offers a practical step for donkeys that will go on to be ridden, as they learn to listen to signals on their body instead of relying on signals up by their head.

You will need two lengths of climbing rope, approximately 6–7m long (depending on the size of your donkey), a wand, and an assistant who can lead your donkey while you introduce the ropes and work through the steps to chest line driving.

Note the position of the donkey's ear as he listens to the assistant who is giving the verbal cues.

Considerations

Teach the 'walking up from behind' exercise first to break down this lesson into small easy-to-process steps and show your assistant how to ask your donkey to walk on, slow down and halt without pulling on the lead line. They will need to keep ahead of your donkey's nose to avoid tripping you up when you introduce the rope.

How to

Start with your assistant leading your donkey from his near side. With the rope around the donkey's neck, hold the rope with both hands and ask your assistant to walk your donkey forwards. This gives your donkey the chance to process the sensation and sight of the rope on,

and extending from, his body. Ask your assistant to halt your donkey. If your donkey cannot walk forwards or stop on cue, it may be a sign of concern.

Remove the rope from his neck and rub it gently over his body. Alternatively you can wrap the rope around a schooling stick and stroke him along his back and barrel and down his hind legs with the wand and the rope.

If your donkey is calm, tie the rope around his neck with a quick-release knot. Ask your assistant to invite him to walk forwards using a wand or their arm, and a gentle ask-and-release signal on the lead line if necessary. You can give the verbal cue 'and walk' to accustom the donkey to listen to your voice and not only focus on the leader.

Attach the second line and tie both lines together around the neck using the tail ends of the rope on both sides.

As your donkey walks forwards, gradually fall back but keep out to the side so that your donkey can clearly see you in his peripheral vision. Initially, do not allow the rope to make contact with his flank. When your donkey is settled, you can move nearer to him so that the rope gently touches his side.

Follow the track of his inside hind leg and ensure that your assistant only turns him to the left if you are both on his near side. If your helper turns him to the right you may be placed in a vulnerable position and the rope may cross your donkey's hind legs, which might make him panic.

It is not possible for you to turn your donkey purely from the chest line but you can ask him to slow down and halt using an ask-and-release signal with the rope. To ask him

Make a bridge with the rope between your hands to maintain a stable connection.

to walk on, gently scoop the rope upwards against his flank as you give him the verbal cue 'and walk'.

Once your donkey is confidently walking forwards, slowing and stopping from signals with the chest line and your voice, you can repeat the exercise with the single rope on his other side, again working through each step. Remember your assistant will also need to switch sides.

Build on this exercise by attaching both single lengths of rope around his neck. Ensure you tie them together using the 'tails' from each rope. Start with both lines on one side. If your donkey is calm and able to walk, slow and halt on cue, deftly flip one line over his back and create a bridge with the ropes as shown. If working on a circle, follow the track of his inside hind on the turns.

73. Noises from behind

Noises behind an animal can trigger a natural startle response. In some cases this can be linked to tension through the hindquarters. Although generally more common in timid donkeys, unexpected sounds can take even the most confident donkey by surprise.

As well as being appropriate for every donkey, this exercise is particularly important if he is going to be trained under saddle or driven. If driving is to be a safe and enjoyable experience for all concerned, it is imperative that the donkey becomes accustomed to the constant noise from the cart or carriage and does not panic if the sounds change as the wheels pass over different surfaces, such as drain covers, or if brambles or branches get snagged on any part of the vehicle.

This exercise is a natural progression from chest line driving and walking up from behind. Although all the TTouch body-work and ground-work exercises can help to reduce noise sensitivity without necessarily needing

to teach such a specific skill, it is well worth adding this lesson into the donkey's general education.

Considerations

You will need an assistant, a 2m length of rope and some plastic soda or water bottles. If your donkey is excessively or consistently noise sensitive, you may need to rule out possible underlying medical problems that could be contributing to this behaviour. As with the other ground-work exercises, work at a pace that is comfortable for your donkey and observe his reactions at all times.

How to

Start by tying a single plastic bottle to the length of rope and ask your assistant to hold the rope in one hand. To begin with, he must stand still while you lead your donkey around so that he can observe the assistant and the equipment from a distance that he feels is safe. Ask your donkey to stand and walk on using your verbal cues, and gradually lead him closer until he is able to walk confidently around your assistant. Observe your donkey's reactions at all times. When he is settled, lead him away to a safe distance and ask him to halt facing your assistant.

Ask your assistant to gently raise and lower the rope so that the donkey becomes accustomed to the movement of the bottle. If your donkey remains calm, ask your assistant to lower the rope so that the container comes into contact with the ground, and then walk for a few paces with it dragging behind them. If your donkey shows any signs of concern, ask your assistant to stop.

Remember to go back a stage if necessary at any point and gradually build up the complexity of the exercise in small, achievable steps. If your donkey remains calm as your helper drags the bottle at a distance, invite your donkey to move as well but ensure that you remain at an acceptable distance from your assistant.

Serpentine your donkey as you walk parallel to your helper so that he begins to approach, then turn away from the noise. Gradually decrease the distance between you and your assistant as appropriate and increase the depth of the serpentine loops.

Once your donkey is happily walking towards and away from the helper, ask him to start following your donkey. If your donkey shows any signs of concern, ask your assistant to slow down or stop and go back a step or give the donkey a break.

Tie additional bottles to the rope as your donkey develops more confidence, but remember to work in stages. Every new bottle will change the appearance and sound of the moving rope. When your donkey is able to walk calmly forwards and halt on cue as your handler drags the rope and bottles behind him, teach him the same exercise while he is wearing his bridle if you intend to drive him in blinkers.

Build in small steps, adding more containers one by one, and ensure that the donkey remains calm at every stage.

74. Walking under wands

Teaching a donkey to walk under raised wands is another TTouch foundation exercise that can help address loading problems, build confidence and prepare a donkey to walk under low hanging branches on tracks, bridle paths or down country lanes. It is a practical exercise to teach donkeys that will go on to be ridden or driven as it helps them to become accustomed to the sight of something taller than a person standing on the ground over their back as well as behind them.

Considerations

You will need two helpers, two long dressage schooling sticks, two blocks (unless your donkey is small) and some treats. As with every exercise,

avoid rushing through the stages and break the sessions down into small steps over several days if necessary.

Teach the donkey to walk through narrow gaps and accustom him to being stroked all over his body with a wand before progressing to this exercise.

How to

Set two plastic blocks or bales of bedding, hay or straw parallel to each other and walk your donkey through the gap. There needs to be enough distance between the bales for you and your donkey to walk between them but they must not be so far apart that the wands will not meet when your assistants are standing on the blocks with their wands held up in the air.

Ask your donkey to stand between the bales and then halt on the other side. If he cannot stop at either point, he is concerned. If he is worried by the narrow gap, increase the space until he is confidently walking through the gap and then decrease the space once more.

Ask your handlers to stand next to the blocks holding a wand upright in their hands. If your donkey is worried by the sight of the wands, your assistants can hold them by their sides with the button end close to, or on the ground.

Lead your donkey through the gap and

remember to ask him to stand and halt between and after passing your helpers. If he rushes or freezes, the assistants can offer him a little treat one at a time to build his confidence. If he cannot eat, it is a sign that his concerns are escalating so stop the exercise and give him a break and remember to go back a few steps when you start again.

If your donkey is calmly walking past your assistants, ask them to raise the wands in the air with the ends pointing straight upwards. Lead your donkey through the gap from both sides and ask him to stop as before. Allow him time to explore your friends and the wands if he wishes to engage with them before quietly walking on.

Your assistants can then stand on the bales one at a time, first with the wands pointing upwards then with one angled slightly towards

Ask the donkey to halt before walking him past your assistants, and give him time to observe the handlers and any equipment that is being used in this exercise.

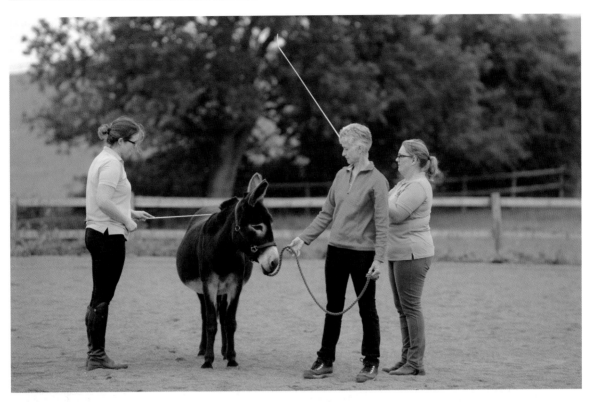

Once your donkey can walk and halt under two raised wands, ask the assistants to stroke the donkey with their wands one at a time.

the other person. Keep leading your donkey through the set-up but remember he may need time out to process each new experience.

The final stage is to have both assistants standing on the bales with their wands held aloft and angled towards each other so that the tips of the wands meet to create an arch.

As well as you asking your donkey to walk and halt under the arch, your assistants can stroke him with their wands one at a time to teach him that contact from something above is nothing to fear.

75. Walking under low coloured objects and bunting

This is an extension of the previous exercise and can be of benefit for donkeys that are worried

about loading, hesitate before walking under a low door frame, are easily spooked, will be attending fêtes and festive gatherings, and those that will go on to be ridden or driven.

Any new experience builds confidence. Teaching donkeys to walk under coloured objects is a useful exercise as it encourages them to adapt more quickly to new experiences in a known environment, and can be helpful even if you do not intend to take your donkey out and about.

Considerations

Teaching your donkey to walk under wands will help your donkey process this exercise more quickly. It can also be beneficial to teach your donkey to walk over plastic sheeting if you intend to use coloured bunting or anything that might flap in the breeze. You also need to have taught your donkey to walk through a narrow gap as this forms part of this exercise.

Bear in mind that even though you may have diligently worked through every step with a more stable and more neutral object like a dressage schooling stick, your donkey may still need time to process the size, shape and colour of the novel item.

How to

Set up your ground-work exercise as described in the previous section. Coloured pool noodles are ideal for this exercise: they are relatively cheap to buy, easy to handle and come in a variety of colours.

Work through each step listed in the previous exercise, but with your helpers holding pool noodles instead of wands, until your donkey is happily walking through the narrow gap beneath the pool noodle arch. Remember to teach your donkey to halt in front of, in the middle, and after the arch. If he cannot stand quietly or walk forwards on cue, he is concerned.

Once your donkey is happily walking under the arch, ask your handlers to dispense with one pool noodle and hold the other

Hold the coloured pool noodles in the air to form an arch.

Ask your donkey to halt under the low bar and remember to praise him for being the brilliant donkey that he is.

one between them, as high up in the air as possible. Repeat the earlier steps of halting and so on as you walk your donkey under the straight bar.

As your donkey grows in confidence, ask your assistants to gradually lower the pool noodle. Remember to lead your donkey through the exercise from both ends of the set-up. Lower your own body and gently stroke the lead line to encourage the donkey to lower his neck and head as the space between the pool noodle and the ground decreases.

If you want to teach your donkey to walk under bunting, begin by asking your assistants to stand with one foot on one end of a strip of bunting while they hold the other end

in one hand. As before, slowly repeat the steps. As you progress, the bunting can be wrapped around the wands to form the arch. Remember that any breeze may make plastic bunting flap and your donkey may need time to become accustomed to the noise. If he is worried, walk around the outside of the set-up before asking him to stand between your helpers.

Once he is happily standing under the arch, dispense with the wands and ask your assistants to hold the bunting between them, as high as possible at first. Lower the bunting as appropriate and remember to let your donkey know how brilliant he is at every step along the way.

CASE HISTORY

Name: Dora

Age: Three years

Breed: Mixed breed standard jenny

Concern: Worried when handled around the head, timid, and reluctant to be caught

Recipe for success

- Build a bond through quiet, consistent interactions in the stable on arrival in her new home.
- Note any tension around the base of the donkey's ears and use warm towels to loosen matted hair and debris on the ears.
- Turn out in small grassy paddock and hang out on other side of the fence and in the paddock without initiating contact.
- Once the donkey is happily remaining grazing while being admired from a safe distance, carry two white dressage schooling sticks into paddock and slowly move them in the air.
- Slowly guide the donkey across the pasture with the two white wands but stop the moment she quickens her pace.
- Repeat the above steps in small sessions throughout the afternoon until the donkey can be quietly ushered towards the gate.
- Once the donkey is calmly standing while contained with the wands, use one wand to stroke the brave donkey on her chocolate-coloured chest.
- Use the second wand to stroke her gently along her back.
- Avoid the temptation to take her by the headcollar in case she overcooks.
- Let her rest.
- Repeat the steps once more and gently lay a rope over the top of her neck.
- Stroke the brilliant donkey with the back of the hand and quietly slide the rope around her neck.
- Pause and let her process every new ingredient.
- Slowly clip the rope to the headcollar and let the little donkey know how brave and beautiful she is.
- Note that the donkey cannot eat once the lead line is on her headcollar and walk her quietly back to her stable.
- Practise over several days keeping to the same quiet routine and continuing with gentle body-work in the safety of the stall.
- Marvel as the little donkey begins to learn it is safe for her to graze in-hand on her way back to the yard.
- Resist the temptation to scream and shout with joy when the donkey first calls out to you and comes trotting over when she sees you walking towards her field – and whisper 'you are wonderful' instead.

CASE HISTORY

Names: JJ and Bridget

Age: Four years

Breed: Miniature Mediterranean

Concern: Both donkeys became worried when attempts were made to take the more confident JJ out for a walk and separate the bonded pair for short periods, even though Bridget had the company of a miniature pony when left at home

Recipe for success

- Start by interacting with both donkeys at liberty in a familiar enclosure to build confidence through giving them control and choice.
- Observe their responses while talking to the guardian and note that the donkeys had had little experience of change within their home environment.
- Gradually introduce novel items one object at a time over several sessions and reward each donkey for even the quickest glance at the surface, container or toy with small slices of carrot and lots of verbal praise.
- Bring in folded towels, a cardboard box and then a ball, and mix in gentle scratches and verbal praise as the donkeys interact with all the objects.
- Once the donkeys are happily exploring all the items, extend the exercise by moving the surfaces and toys to an area outside their yard.
- Note when the donkeys started to increase the distance between them when grazing as their confidence levels began to rise.
- Introduce leading exercises, clipping the rope to the side of the headcollar and ensure the line is free from tension at all times.
- Contain one donkey and walk the second donkey around the yard but be mindful to keep him in sight of his friend at first.
- Keep each session short and sweet.
- Build gradually and extend the length of time and distance between the donkeys as one is being led and the other is standing quietly by. Remember to work with both donkeys in the same rewarding way.
- Relish the moment you can take each donkey out for a quiet walk along the lanes while the other remains happily at home with their miniature equine friend.

CASE HISTORY

Name: Ted

Age: Six years

Breed: Mixed breed gelding

Concern: Sensitive to contact on and around his ears

Recipe for success

- Note which ear triggers the most concern and begin on the side that is less worrying for your donkey friend.
- Start by using the Zebra TTouch over his withers and gradually zigzag your hand up the side of his neck towards his ear and back down.
- Pause between movements to allow the donkey to respond and process this different connection.
- Once the donkey starts to enjoy the rewarding contact on his neck, gently cup the base of his ear with the side of your hand.
- Move your hand in slow circles to move his ear.
- Remember to give him plenty of breaks.
- Stroke the ear from the base to the tip and marvel as the contented donkey begins to lower his head.
- Apply the same techniques to the donkey's more sensitive ear.

CASE HISTORY

Name: Tom

Age: Three years old

Breed: Mixed breed standard donkey

Concern: Kicking out or walking off when asked to pick up a leg

Recipe for success

- Introduce a wand and stroke the donkey first down his front legs and then his hind limbs.
- Pause between each leg to enable the donkey to process what you are asking him to do.
- Once the donkey is able to settle as you stroke his legs with the wand, use the back of your hand to touch him on the shoulder.
- Remove your hand the moment he turns his head away.
- Let him rest.
- Repeat the steps and quietly lay the back of your hand on his shoulder once more.
- Observe the donkey's response.
- When he is settled, gradually slide the back of your hand down the upper part of his foreleg and remove your hand before you reach his knee.
- Build over several sessions as necessary until you can stroke him all the way down to his hoof.
- Use wither rocks to show the donkey how to transfer his weight from side to side.
- Slide the palm of your hand down his foreleg and gently scratch him on the back of his fetlock.
- When he picks up his foot praise him but do not attempt to hold his hoof.
- Let him rest.
- Build gradually until the clever donkey can lift each foot in turn when he feels the gentle scratch on the back of each fetlock.
- Support the hoof with one hand and ensure it is not lifted higher than the donkey's knee and is not pulled out to the side.
- Keep the toe pointing towards the ground and gently pick out the foot.
- Repeat the same techniques with the other front foot and remember to give the donkey plenty of breaks.
- Once he can easily lift each front leg on cue, use Zebra TTouches along the donkey's back and follow the same steps to access and then lift each hind limb.
- Enjoy the ease with which you are able to pick out your donkey's hooves while he stands calmly in the field.

Useful Contacts and Resources

Tellington TTouch UK:
www.ttouch.co.uk

Tellington TTouch USA:
www.ttouch.com

Tellington TTouch Canada:
www.ttouch.ca

Connected Riding:
www.connectedriding.com

The Donkey Sanctuary:
www.thedonkeysanctuary.org.uk

RSPCA Lockwood Centre for Horses and Donkeys:
www.rspca.org.uk/lockwood

Nowzad:
www.nowzad.com

Further Reading and References

FURTHER READING

Byard, Jack, *Know your Donkeys and Mules* (Old Pond Publishing)
Ellis, Vivian, Ellis, Richard and Claxton, Joy, *Donkey Driving* (J.A. Allen)
Morris, Dorothy and Sims, Rob, *Looking After a Donkey* (Whittet Books)
Svendsen, Elisabeth C., *The Professional Handbook of the Donkey* (Donkey Sanctuary)
Weaver, Sue, *The Donkey Companion – Selecting, training, breeding, enjoying and caring for donkeys* (Storey Publishing)

REFERENCES

Kimura *et al.*, 'Ancient DNA from Nubian and Somali wild ass provides insights into donkey ancestry and domestication' in Gepts, Paul (ed.) *Biodiversity in Agriculture* (Cambridge University Press)
Marshall, Fiona B. *et al.* 'Evaluating the Roles of Directed Breeding and Gene Flow in Animal Domestication' in Proceedings of the National Academy of Sciences, USA
Goleman, Daniel, 1996, *Emotional Intelligence* (Bloomsbury)
Rischkowsky & Pilling, 2007 'The State of the World's Animal Genetic Resources for Food and Agriculture' (Commission on Genetic Resources for Food and Agriculture)
Valberg & Macleay n.d., in Geor, R.J. *et al. Equine Applied and Clinical Nutrition: Health, Welfare and Performance* (Saunders Elsevier),

Acknowledgements

RSPCA Lockwood Centre for Horses and Donkeys
Bob Atkins
Mags Denness
Shelley Hawkins
Vicki McGarva
Linda Tellington Jones
Peggy Cummings
Robyn Hood
Mandy Pretty
Natalie Tindall
Tanya Lynn and David Smith
Mr Pinkerton, Pink Floyd, Poppy, Willow, Dora, Maybelle, Tilly and the donkeys at the RSPCA
    Lockwood Centre for Horses and Donkeys
Dr Mujtaba, Jalala and the team at Nowzad

Index